Inside the E

Taoiseach Jack Lynch and Dr Patrick Hillery, Minister for External Affairs, sign the Treaty of Accession in 1972, enabling Ireland to join the European Communities.

Inside the EEC

AN IRISH GUIDE

Ruth Barrington
&
John Cooney

Cartoons by Martyn Turner

THE O'BRIEN PRESS

DUBLIN

First published 1984 by The O'Brien Press Ltd.
20 Victoria Road   Dublin 6   Ireland
© copyright reserved
Ruth Barrington & John Cooney

British Library Cataloguing in Publication Data
Barrington, Ruth
Inside the EEC.
1. European Economic Community
I. Title   II. Cooney, John
341.24'22   HC241.2
ISBN 0-86278-057-8 hardback
ISBN 0-86278-058-6 paperback

Acknowledgements
We wish to thank the following for use of photographs: *The
Irish Times* pp. 1, 112, 119, 125, 172; Pacemaker p. 104; Pat
Langan p. 99; Richard Mills p. 160; Bord Failte p. 139.

Cover design by Michael O'Brien and Frances Hyland.
Symbol by Donald McDonald.
Photograph of authors by Pat Langan.
Edited by Íde ní Laoghaire.
Typeset by Computer Graphics Ltd.
Printed by O'Brien Promotions, Dublin.

Contents

Abbreviations

ACP African, Caribbean and Pacific countries party to the Lomé Convention

ASEAN Association of South-East Asian Nations

CCT Common Customs Tariff

COREPER Committee of Permanent Representatives (attached to Council of Ministers)

DG Directorate General (Department of the Commission)

EDF European Development Fund

EFTA European Free Trade Association

EIB European Investment Bank

EMS European Monetary System

EMU European Monetary Union

ERDF European Regional Development Fund

FEOGA European Agricultural Guidance and Guarantee Fund

GATT General Agreement on Tariffs and Trade (United Nations)

GSP Generalised System of Preferences

IMF International Monetary Fund

MCA Monetary Compensatory Amount

NATO North Atlantic Treaty Organisation

NCI New Community Instrument (for loans)

NGO Non-governmental Organisation

OECD Organisation for Economic Co-operation and Development

OEEC Organisation for European Economic Cooperation

STABEX System for the Stabilisation of ACP Export Earnings

UNCTAD United Nations Conference on Trade and Development

VAT Value Added Tax

IR£ = Irish pounds; £ = sterling.

Acknowledgements

Many people helped us with the preparation of *Inside the EEC*. We would like to thank Tom and Aine Barrington who inspired this unlikely partnership. We received invaluable assistance from those who commented on chapters in draft form or suggested ideas: Donal Barrington, Paul Cullen, Tom Gaffney, Peter Grant, John Healy, Denis Maher, Maurice Manning, Lucy McCaffrey, Geoff Martin, Ken O'Brien, Norah O'Neill, John O'Toole, John Sexton, Dermot Scott, Mary Sutton and others. The authors, however, are responsible for all opinions and interpretations in the text. Conor Maguire, Peter Doyle, Tim Kelly and the staff of the Dublin Office of the Commission of the European Communities were particularly helpful. We are grateful to the Commission and *The Irish Times* for photographs, to Martyn Turner for adding his distinctive angle on Community affairs, to Pat Langan for the publicity photographs and to Liz Meldon who typed much of the text. Michael O'Brien and Ide ní Laoghaire encouraged us by their enthusiasm and commitment to the project. We are also aware of the debt we owe to Liguori Barrins and John Delap who good humouredly surrendered us on Saturdays so that we could write this guide. We dedicate the book to them and to a young European, Francis Cooney.

Ruth Barrington & John Cooney

Prologue

31 December 1972 In a remote part of south Kerry, local people make their way to the holiday home of a Dublin family to celebrate the new year. At midnight, as the Dubliners strike up 'Auld Lang Syne', the Kerrymen cheer the start of a new era: 'Here's to the Common Market,' they exclaim, 'now we are all Europeans.'

7 June 1979 For the first time since the 1918 general election voters on both sides of the border go to the polling booths with the same purpose. They are voting not for Irish unity nor the maintenance of the union with Britain; they are electing representatives to a multinational parliament dedicated to the creation of a united Europe.

17 July 1979 'You write the date-line in full because if it isn't quite twenty-four hours old it is already in the history books of Europe with Armistice Day, and D-Day and V-Day. And it is in a way the sum of these days, as men and women come to this town in recognition of the old simple fact that, as a national Parliament is a substitute for civil war, so a supranational Parliament will hopefully be a substitute for supracivil war.' John Healy, reporting from Strasbourg on the opening session of the first directly elected European Parliament.

Three glimpses of the euphoric and symbolic impact of EEC membership on Ireland. Although Irish saints and scholars played their part in medieval Europe, in later centuries the island was dominated and divided by its bigger neighbour, Britain. Indeed, Britain's entry to the European Community along with Ireland was seen as providing an historic opportunity to create a more equal relationship between the two islands and to bring peace to Northern Ireland in the spirit of the post-war Franco-German reconciliation.

Twelve years later, much of the optimism of membership has gone as Ireland comes to terms with the crippling super-levy on milk, as Britain's demands for budget reform threaten the basis of Community finance and as unemployment disillusions many about the material gains of EEC membership. What has happened to the farming bonanza of the mid-1970s? Why were the regional and social funds so disappointing? Was the break with sterling and the link with the stronger European currencies a mistake? What has been the contribution in Europe of Irish ministers, commissioners,

7

European Parliament members and civil servants? Has European membership compromised Ireland's neutrality?

These, and other questions, loom large in Irish society and politics at the time of writing as European elections beckon the public again and as Ireland takes over the presidency of the EEC for the second half of 1984. As a contribution to the public debate we have tried to put these questions into the context of how the EEC institutions operate and how the policies work.

Athens, December 1983: the European Council ends in disarray.

8

1
Community Building

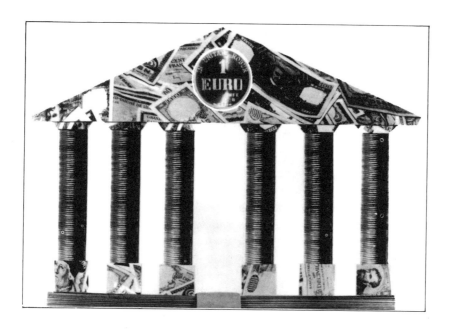

IF THE NINETEENTH CENTURY in Europe was dominated by nationalism as the predominant philosophy of government, it also nurtured the competing ideal of an organised Europe. After the failure of Napoleon to subject Europe to France's interests, a French social theorist, Henri de Saint Simon, wrote a book in 1814 on *The Social Reorganisation of European Society*, arguing for the need to bring the peoples of Europe together in a single political body while conserving the national independence of each of them. And at a peace conference in Paris in 1849, writer Victor Hugo spoke of 'a united states of Europe' which would end warfare. 'You will have many more quarrels to settle, interests to discuss, arguments to resolve, but do you realise what you will substitute for men-at-arms, guns, lances, pikes and swords? - a little wooden box which you will call the ballot box,' he predicted.

These were no more than ideals in a world in which war became more savage. After the horrors of the First World War, 1914-18, which undermined Europe's supremacy in the world, the League of Nations was set up to maintain peace. Ireland joined the League in 1930 shortly after France's Foreign Minister Aristide Briand had proposed the establishment of 'a system for a European federal union'. While member states would retain their economic and political sovereignty, they would belong to the new joint institutions of a European Conference, a Permanent Political Committee and a Secretariat. Geneva would be the location for the European Federation.

The positive response of the Irish government to the Briand proposal was described by the influential quarterly journal, *The Round Table*, as 'the most important diplomatic document' to have emerged from the Department of External Affairs. In 1932 Eamon de Valera, as President of the Council of the League, failed to obtain support for the plan. According to historian Dermot Keogh, de Valera at that time believed that 'some surrender of national sovereignty was essential in order to resolve disputes through the machinery of international law'. (See Keogh, Further Reading p. 186).

Dismissed by Britain as 'vague and puzzling idealism', the Briand plan today attracts notice as a missed opportunity. Economic depression provided the conditions for Hitler's rise to power in Germany and it was not until after the Second World War that determined efforts were made to translate the supranational ideal into a reality. A high point in this movement was the Congress of Europe that took place in The Hague in May 1948, bringing together representatives and observers from twenty-five countries, including a delegation from Ireland which consisted of Senator James Douglas, Professor Michael Tierney and Senator Eleanor Butler. The meeting, dominated by Winston Churchill and the British Conservatives, led to the formation of the European Movement and to the setting up in 1949 of the Council of Europe. Sean MacBride, the Irish representative, remains the sole surviving founder member.

Although Churchill had, in Zurich in 1946, called for 'a united states of Europe', the key British figure in post-war Europe was the Labour Foreign Secretary Ernest Bevin. It was Bevin who organised the European response to the offer of American aid from the US Secretary of State General George Marshall and it was Bevin who was the architect of the North Atlantic Treaty Organisation (NATO) that tied the Americans to the defence of Europe. But it should be stressed that so keen was the United States for European integration that it was prepared to pay an economic price for the development of a strong and prosperous western Europe - through Marshall Aid (from which Ireland received £47 million) and by helping a major competitor in trade - the EEC - to develop.

While Britain was prepared to lend its weight to restore European strength, it was unwilling to go further and cede sovereignty in moves to integrate the economies of European states. Such moves were initiated by the French under the influence of a brilliant technocrat, Jean Monnet, who believed that the key to peace in western Europe was through economic integration and the creation of supranational institutions with power to act in the common interest. The former brandy salesman from the town of Cognac convinced the French Foreign Minister Robert Schuman of the importance of a supranational initiative.

At an historic news conference in the Quai d'Orsay in Paris on 9 May 1950 Schuman called for the ending of Franco-German rivalry through 'a constructive act' rather than with 'vain words'. He proposed that the coal and steel production of France and Germany be pooled under the administration of a new 'high authority' whose decisions would be binding.

Schuman saw this offer as a first step towards the creation of an economic community and as laying 'the first concrete foundations of the European Federation which is indispensable to the maintenance of peace'. The Schuman declaration was welcomed by Chancellor Konrad Adenauer. Germany had made a remarkable economic recovery but it was still treated as a conquered and partitioned power whose revival might yet again threaten the peace of its neighbours. A particular threat was posed by the huge German iron and steel firms of the Ruhr, which were at the centre of the conflict that had led to the two world wars. Fearful of future German dominance, the French turned to the supranational solution as the way of maintaining peace and thus of ensuring that Europe would be strong vis-à-vis the Soviet Union and the United States. The Schuman declaration, therefore, brought Germany out of its isolation, restoring its political independence while providing a strong buffer against Soviet expansionism. Italy, anxious for rehabilitation after the rule of Mussolini and Fascism, responded eagerly. The Benelux countries, which had already established their own customs union, were hesitant when they saw Britain's indifference but they responded favourably when a decision was required. The negotiations, begun in June 1950, were completed ten months later with the signing on 18 April 1951 of the Treaty of Paris, establishing the European Coal and Steel Community. After ratification by the six national parliaments this treaty came into force on 25 July 1952.

With the tide towards unity so strong, consideration was given next to the formation of a European Defence Community and a European Political Community. The vulnerability of Europe had been revealed in 1951 when it was feared that the Russians might launch an attack while the United States was fighting in Korea. The problem was how to strengthen Europe without raising strong national armies, especially in Germany. France proposed a limited German rearmament as part of a European army owing allegiance to a European Defence Community. In order to keep a democratic check on the military, a further proposal was made that Europe's defence would be the political responsibility of a European organisation consisting of a directly elected people's chamber and an indirectly elected senate, as well as a European executive council responsible to a parliament, a council of ministers and a court of justice. A treaty establishing these two communities was signed by the Six in 1952, but to make the communities operative a unanimous vote was required in all the national parliaments. The Defence Community was aborted in 1954 when the French National Assembly rejected it. The political union scheme, essential to a defence community, also lapsed.

Despite this set-back, renewed efforts were made to extend cooperation on economic matters and nuclear energy based on the model of the Coal and Steel Community. A meeting of foreign ministers of the Six at Messina, Sicily, in June 1955 resulted in proposals for a customs union and a common market. The French, fearful that free trade in industrial goods might damage their highly protected industry, secured compensatory agreement from the Germans for the development of a common agricultural policy. The British attended the preliminary negotiations but later withdrew.

The two treaties establishing the European Economic Community and the European Atomic Energy Community were signed in Rome on 25 March 1957. They were approved by the six national parliaments and came into force on 1 January 1958, with Brussels as the headquarters for the three communities. The Rome Treaty established a European Commission and a Council of Ministers as well as a European Assembly and a Court of Justice. The Commission was to propose policies and legislation and the Council of Ministers was to take decisions primarily by majority votes. Rapid progress was made by the institutions in removing customs barriers, cutting tariffs, integrating economies, allowing free circulation of people and goods, and in creating the common agricultural policy.

The apparent headlong rush towards supranationalism was checked dramatically however in the lofty person of France's General Charles de Gaulle. On coming to power in 1958 the General accepted the Common Market as a fait accompli but he did not conceal his dislike for it, describing the aim of 'L'Europe des Peuples' as 'an artificial motherland' and as 'the brain-child of the technocrats'. Rather than a federal Europe he believed in 'L'Europe des Patries'. Determined to change the character of the Community, the General proposed, to Chancellor Adenauer in 1960, a European political union with new institutions that would provide for periodic meetings of the heads of government and their foreign ministers.

There would be a permanent political secretariat, four permanent committees dealing with foreign policy, defence, economics and culture and a European assembly appointed by national governments. These proposals, known as the 'Fouchet plan', ran into opposition from the smaller member states and were abandoned in 1962.

Because of the failure of his political scheme de Gaulle's dislike of the Community increased. He chose a conflict with the first President of the Commission Walter Hallstein, an aloof and ambitious German who saw himself cast in the role of prime minister of a new united Europe. In his haste to acquire more powers for the Commission, Hallstein put forward proposals, as envisaged in the Treaties, for the direct financing of the Community by giving it the power to collect proceeds from levies and import duties. Before facing the Council of Ministers, Hallstein won the support of the European Assembly which was itself seeking a say in the fixing of revenue. This leap towards federalism was thwarted when France's Foreign Minister Couve de Murville not only objected to the proposals but withdrew French ministers and officials from meetings of the Council of Ministers on the order of de Gaulle. For six months this 'empty chair' policy was sustained by France until in January 1966 a compromise was reached in Luxembourg, limiting the exercise of majority voting in the Council. 'When very important matters are at stake', the Luxembourg compromise stipulated, 'discussion must continue until unanimous agreement is reached'. In practice, member states could now plead that a vital national interest was at stake when faced with proposals they did not like. Thus, the Commission's power to initiate legislation was subtly diminished by the French requirement that the Commission should consult member states 'at the appropriate level before submitting proposals for Community action of particular importance to the Council'. The empty chair, wrote Jean Lecerf in *La Communauté en Péril*, profoundly changed the rules of the Community.

Meanwhile, the economic success of the Community impressed the British who were taking stock of their post-colonial decline and were finding the possibility of access to the expanding common market more attractive. Such a reappraisal by Britain held significant implications for those countries dependent on the British market, such as Ireland, Denmark and Norway. It was a major consideration for Ireland, 74% of whose exports went to Britain in 1960. Like Britain, Ireland was a founder member in 1948 of the Organisation for European Economic Cooperation (OEEC) and was, along with Britain, one of the original ten members of the Strasbourg-based Council of Europe. Unlike Britain, however, Ireland did not join the North Atlantic Treaty Organisation (NATO), refusing, in the words of the Minister for External Affairs Sean MacBride to join 'any military alliance with, or commitment involving military action jointly with, the State that is responsible for the unnatural division of Ireland'.

MacBride's declaration was an application of Eamon de Valera's wartime policy of neutrality, but it was de Valera's successor Seán Lemass who modified this stance in respect of European Community membership when he realised that by the late 1950s the world trend was towards free trade and that Ireland had to reduce the protective measures enacted since 1932. Indeed, an abortive plan of 1957-8 to merge the common market with the OEEC in a European free trade area brought Ireland face to face with the prospect of free trade and lent urgency to the task of modernising the structure of the Irish economy.

In 1960 Ireland opened exploratory talks with the General Agreement on Tariffs and Trade (GATT) and on 31 July 1961 applied for EEC membership, narrowly ahead of an application from Britain. In preliminary talks with EEC foreign ministers in Brussels in January 1962 Lemass explained that Ireland's application represented not only a deliberate decision on the part of the government but also corresponded with the sentiments of the Irish people. Regarding the political aims of the Community, he said that, while Ireland had not joined NATO, it had always agreed with NATO's general aims. The fact that Ireland had not joined was due to special circumstances (partition) but this did not diminish Ireland's acceptance of the goal of European unity. The Irish government, he said, would energetically promote the adaptation of Irish industry to common market conditions. Of particular interest to Ireland was the Commission's proposals for a common agricultural policy. 'We are, naturally, anxious that, through membership of the European Economic Community, Ireland should be able to look forward to a balanced development of agriculture and industry', Lemass concluded.

The Community opened negotiations with Britain which posed bigger problems of adaptation to Community rules, but these negotiations were halted by a veto from de Gaulle on the grounds that Britain was not ready for membership. Ireland's application, along with those of Denmark and Norway, remained 'on the table'. All four applications were reactivated in 1967 when Prime Minister Harold Wilson applied for a second time, but the General again said no.

This setback was used to advantage by Ireland with the signing in 1965 of the Anglo-Irish Free Trade Agreement which marked an important step away from protectionism, and in 1967 Ireland joined GATT. While Lemass was paving the Republic's road to EEC membership, Northern Ireland remained sullenly silent on the prospect of joining the Community — perceived as an invention of Roman Catholic Christian Democrats such as Adenauer and Italy's Alicide de Gasperi. It was not without significance in the Unionist mind that the fundamental constitution of the EEC was the Treaty of Rome. Without challenge in 1957, Lord Glentoran could assure the Stormont Parliament in Belfast that there was no need for a committee to study the possible effects on Northern Irish industry of the common market. Even more insularly, Herbert Kirk pronounced that 'whatever was finally decided for the good of the United Kingdom it followed that, on balance, it was good for Ulster'.

A new horizon opened up in 1968 with the resignation of General de Gaulle. The European debut of his successor Georges Pompidou coincided in The Hague in December 1969 with that of Chancellor Willy Brandt of West Germany. With both leaders eager to make an impression, The Hague summit provided the green light for the resumption of the accession negotiations with the four applicant countries, revived the aim of economic and political union and, reflecting the more radical mood of the latter 1960s, emphasised the importance of social affairs. Reacting against the image of the common market as 'the rich man's club', Pompidou said that Europe must not become a community of tradesmen, while Brandt called for 'a human face' to the community.

On 30 June 1970 the Irish tricolour and the union jack flew alongside each other and the flags of the other member states in Luxembourg. The Irish delegation, consisting of Sean Morrissey of the Department of External Affairs, Denis Maher of Finance, James O'Mahony of Agriculture and Desmond Culligan of Industry and Commerce, was led by Foreign Minister Patrick Hillery. To advance Ireland's case, Taoiseach Jack Lynch toured the capitals of the Six. Northern Ireland's interests in the negotiations with Brussels were not represented directly by Stormont ministers but by Whitehall civil servants and British ministers.

Ireland negotiated a four-year transition period for abolishing industrial tariffs and adapting to the common external tariff. Farmers would immediately benefit from higher EEC prices and export subsidies although the price alignment would stretch over five years. The motor assembly industry was given special protection until the end of 1984. An acknowledgement of the importance of promoting Irish economic and industrial development was contained in a special protocol. Difficulties for both Ireland and Britain arose in fishery talks but a compromise was reached allowing existing fishing limits to last for a further decade before being subject to review. Ireland and Britain accepted the treaties and decisions taken by the Six since 1952.

The Treaty of Accession was signed on 22 January 1972 by Ireland, Britain, Denmark and Norway, but in a referendum later that year the Norwegian people rejected the terms of membership and Norway did not join. In contrast, the referendum in Ireland in May recorded a resounding

83.1% vote in favour, with 16.9% against the proposed entry.

A mood of expectancy seized not only Ireland but also the enlarged Community of Nine. High expectations were expressed at the Paris summit of October 1972 when Mr. Lynch, British Prime Minister Edward Heath and the Danish Premier Anker Joergensen joined the leaders of the Six in fixing 1980 as the date for achieving European unity. To check the tendency for capital to gravitate beyond national boundaries to the wealthier regions in an economic and monetary union, a regional fund, proposed by Ireland, Britain and Italy, was to be created by the end of 1973. Vigorous action in the social sphere was to be taken to win popular support for the Community. There would be greater worker participation in industry and in economic and social decisions of the Community. Action programmes were to be formulated for industry, the environment, energy and consumer protection. Ironically however, individuals would still need a national passport to move around the new Europe.

The declaration of the Paris summit may appear to be utopian but the heads of government did not know that they were approaching the end of the post-war era of economic growth and that events would soon be outside their control. A three-letter word sabotaged their efforts: oil. Within a year the Arab-Israeli war broke out resulting in an oil-sale embargo by the Organisation of Petroleum Exporting Countries (OPEC) that caused oil prices to rise fourfold and threw the western economies into the most sustained recession since the 1920s. Europe left the era of prosperity behind and struggled to cope with high inflation, monetary instability and rising unemployment. Regional finance was much lower than expected, social policy was not geared to unemployment and other policy developments were disappointing. Despite this a regional development fund was set up in 1975 and Dr. Hillery, as Social Affairs Commissioner, won support for a social action programme. Although little progress was made towards economic union, the Community provided the framework for containing protectionism. The inter-dependence of the member states was reaffirmed by the presence of the president of the Commission at the annual economic summits of the western industrial nations.

A major institutional development was the decision in 1974 to hold three meetings a year of European leaders — the heads of government and the French President. The European Council, as it was named, was created at the instigation of President Giscard d'Estaing who achieved what de Gaulle had failed to do and what Pompidou had appeared to abandon: the effective subordination of the Commission and the Council of Ministers to the heads of government. Political cooperation and the coordination of EEC policy on international issues by the foreign ministers and diplomats of the member states also increased in importance. Thus, inter-governmental coordination coexisted with Community institutionalism.

In recent years the Community has been dominated by the related questions of Britain's contributions to the budget, the scaling down of farm expenditure, the development of other policies and the need for new budgetary resources. The failure of the Athens and Brussels European Councils in December 1983 and March 1984 highlighted the urgency and complexity of these problems — so much so that in a speech in The Hague President François Mitterrand of France described the Community as a half-abandoned building site.

On the credit side, the European Parliament is now directly elected by universal suffrage, a European monetary system (EMS) came into operation in 1979, Greece became the tenth member in January 1981 and negotiations have begun on Spanish and Portuguese membership. The Community, now in its twenty-seventh year, has shown its ability to resolve differences between member states and overcome problems in a spirit of compromise and in the best interests of the Community as a whole.

We have tended in this country to regard all skulduggery as being acceptable if it comes to getting a grant, a blue card, a summons fixed or an unearned dole from that big faraway entity known as the 'Government'. This tendency has naturally been accentuated when one substitutes the even more faraway concept 'Brussels' for the 'Government' . . . This country needs a directional shift in the organisation of its people and its resources so that we won't be left standing on the periphery of Western Europe, begging bowl extended towards Brussels.   *Irish Press,* 28 January 1984

2
The Anatomy of the EEC

The Palais d'Europe, Strasbourg home of the European Parliament.

The European Community is unique in national and international law. It is neither a state, nor a federation, nor an international organisation, nor a confederation, but is composed of elements of all these. The member states remain the masters of the Community, yet the Community has the authority, in areas where it is competent, to bind member states. The unique character of the Community stems from: its organisation, what it does and how it makes law.

Organisation

The Community was designed to reconcile the interests of member states through the promotion of ever closer integration between them. Its organisation for the most part is governed by the 248 articles of the Treaty of Rome. The Treaty's relationship to the EEC is similar to that of Bunreacht na hEireann, the Irish constitution, to the Irish state — it serves as a 'constitution' for the Community. It lays down the aims of the Community, the role of the institutions, their relationship to each other, the way in which laws are to be made and policies financed and the manner in which international agreements are to be concluded. Unlike Bunreacht na hEireann it does not include moral prescriptions about the rights of the family, the role of women or the indissolubility of marriage. Because the Community is an 'economic' community, the Treaty goes into great detail about economic matters in a way that the Irish constitution does not.

The Treaty applies for an unlimited period of time. The power to amend its provisions lies with the member states which must ratify amendments in accordance with their own constitutional requirements. In Ireland this means that a new treaty would need to be approved by the Oireachtas (Dáil and Seanad).

The other important treaties which, with the Treaty of Rome, define the legal basis of the Community are: the Merger Treaty, 1965, establishing a single Council and a single Commission for the three European communities; the Budget Treaty - better known as the Luxembourg Treaty - 1970, which amended the budgetary provisions of earlier treaties; the Acts of Accession which admitted Britain, Ireland and Denmark to the three communities on 1 January 1973 and Greece on 1 January 1981; the treaty extending the budgetary powers of the European Parliament, 1975.

Institutions

The Treaty of Rome specifies four institutions in the Community: the Council, the Commission, the Assembly or Parliament, the Court of Justice. It provides for other bodies such as the Court of Auditors, the European Investment Bank, and the Economic and Social Committee which have an important position in the Community but do not enjoy the same status as the four institutions.

The Council is the most important of the four because it takes the decisions. Each country is represented by a minister at a meeting of the Council. Which minister depends on the subject under discussion; if it is agriculture the ministers of agriculture attend, if the Community budget the ministers of finance, and so on. It was originally intended that the Council should reach decisions on most issues by majority vote. The Treaty specifies a system of weighted voting in which each member state is allocated votes according to size: Britain, France, Germany and Italy have ten votes each, Belgium, Greece and the Netherlands have five each, Ireland and Denmark three each, and Luxembourg two. The number of votes totals sixty-three. Council decisions on a qualified majority basis are valid if forty-five votes are cast in favour of a proposal from the Commission, or if a minimum of forty-five votes is cast from at least six member states in other cases. The system is designed to prevent the 'big' member states outvoting the 'small' members or vice versa. In practice, majority voting is seldom used at Council meetings and the ministers reach decisions unanimously — or even more frequently fail to agree. There is an important limitation on the Council's power — it is not free to draft Community law and must pass laws proposed by the Commission.

COREPER

The Council is assisted in its work by the Committee of Permanent Representatives, better known as COREPER, from its French initials. The Irish permanent representative is Andrew O'Rourke, former Secretary of the Department of Foreign Affairs. COREPER also supervises the work of more than a hundred working parties attached to the Council of Ministers. When the Council receives a proposal for legislation from the Commission, a working party consisting of officials from the member states is appointed to iron out any technical problems in the draft before discussion at COREPER and the Council of Ministers.

THE COMMISSION

The Commission is the executive of the EEC and its role is pivotal to the smooth functioning of the Community. In order that policies are devised in the best interests of the 270 million citizens of the member states, the Treaty gives the Commission the right to propose policy and frame legislation for decision by the Council of Ministers. There is great interdependence between the Council and the Commission in the decision-making process of the Community and the peculiar relationship of the two institutions has no parallel in other international organisations.

The Commission's other tasks are to administer the established policies of the Community and to ensure that Community laws are obeyed. Fourteen commissioners are appointed for four-year terms by agreement of the member states, the larger countries nominating two and the smaller, one. On appointment, commissioners take an oath before the Court of Justice that they will not seek nor take instructions from any government or any other body. This helps to ensure that the Commission acts in the best interests of the Community.

The Irish members of the Commission have been Patrick Hillery (1973-76), Richard Burke (1977-80), Michael O'Kennedy (1981-2) and again Mr. Burke from April 1982.

The Parliament is composed of 434 members — fifteen from Ireland and three from Northern Ireland — elected by the people of the Community. It is the only institution in which the ordinary citizens of the member states are directly represented. One of the unique features of the Parliament is that the members do not sit according to nationality but in political groupings which are multi-national. The Parliament does not have the powers of a fully developed parliament but is constantly trying to widen its role. The Treaty gives it the right to be consulted by the Council of Ministers on a wide range of issues and to force the Commission to resign by passing a motion of censure. In the 1970s the Parliament won the right to reject the Community budget and to decide the level of expenditure on some items.

Direct elections to the Parliament in 1979 replaced the earlier system where members were nominated by their national parliaments. Since 1979 the Parliament has shown its determination to become a greater force in Community decision-making but so far its victories have been minor. Advocates of increased powers for the Parliament point to the history of democratic assemblies to show that an institution which initially may be no more than a talking shop can develop into a more powerful force.

THE COURT OF JUSTICE

The Court of Justice of the European Communities in Luxembourg is not to be confused with the European Court of Human Rights of the Council of Europe in Strasbourg nor the United Nations International Court of Human Rights in The Hague. The EEC Court was established under the treaties and its jurisdiction lies within the scope of these treaties. Unlike the Court of Human Rights in Strasbourg, it is not primarily concerned with the fundamental rights of citizens vis-à-vis the state, although it uses principles of natural justice in reaching its decisions. Its task is to ensure that within the Community the rule of law is observed and that Community law is interpreted in the same way in every member state. The Court has eleven judges appointed by the common accord of member states for a term of six years which may be renewed. There is no requirement that there should be a judge from each country but in practice each member state nominates one judge. When the eleventh judgeship was created it was decided that it should rotate between the 'big four' member states - France, Germany, Italy and the United Kingdom. Article 167 stipulates that judges must be 'persons whose independence is beyond doubt and who possess the qualifications required for the appointment to the highest judicial office in their respective countries'. For an Irish person to be appointed, he or she would normally be a member of the Supreme or High Court or at least a very senior barrister. So far there have been two Irish judges in the Court, the late Cearbhall O Dalaigh who was President of the Supreme Court on appointment and Andreas O'Keefe, the current Irish judge, who was previously President of the High Court and ex-officio judge of the Supreme Court.

THE ECONOMIC AND SOCIAL COMMITTEE

Although not a formal institution of the Community, the Economic and Social Committee (ESC) is an important consultative body. Composed of industrialists, farmers, trade unionists, retailers, academics and people representing the general interest, its closest parallel in Ireland is the National Economic and Social Council. Germany, Britain, France and Italy have twenty-four members each; Belgium, Greece and the Netherlands have twelve; Denmark and Ireland nine and Luxembourg six, all appointed for a four-year term. The government of each member state nominates to the Council of Ministers twice as many names as it is allowed members on the Committee. The Council consults the Commission which in turn seeks the views of the interest groups at national level. The selected candidates are then appointed by the Council acting unanimously. This complicated procedure is designed to ensure a broad spectrum of interests on the Committee.

The ESC is modelled on a parliamentary assembly, members sitting not according to nationality but in groups by affiliation. There is an employers' group, a farmers' group and a trade union group. Most of the detailed work of the ESC is done in one of its nine 'sections' or committees, covering agriculture, economic affairs, external relations, etc.

In 1980 Thomas Roseingrave, one of the Irish members, was elected president of the ESC for two years. During his term of office he made the expansion of the Community budget and the regional and social policies priorities of the Committee and drew attention to the impact of the common agricultural policy on rural communities.

The institutions enjoy considerable independence of the governments. Commissioners and judges swear on oath to put the interest of the Community before national or sectional interests. The Commission is answerable under the Treaty not to the Council of Ministers but to the Parliament. Direct elections, by making its members answerable to the electorate of Europe, have increased the Parliament's 'democratic legitimacy'. The Court is autonomous in carrying out its functions. Although the institutions are independent of the member states they depend on each other to carry out their functions. The Council cannot act without a proposal from the Commission, the Parliament must approve the budget before the Council votes the money and the Court ensures that the institutions and policies operate within the law. Each institution needs to develop and maintain good relations with the others.

THE EUROPEAN COUNCIL

Although a constitution describes the formal distribution of power in a political system it may not necessarily mention what in practice are the most influential centres of power. It is often remarked that Bunreacht na hEireann does not mention political parties or the civil service. So it is with the Treaty of Rome. It makes no provision for the heads of government to meet to discuss policy. This was considered to be a gap in the constitution by the French in the late 1960s and they initiated regular meetings of the heads of government from 1969 onwards. In 1974 it was agreed that such meetings should be held three times a year and that they should be called 'The Council of the European Communities'. The Council discusses issues arising directly from the operation of the Community and questions of foreign policy affecting the Ten in the context of political cooperation. It has become central to the working of the Community.

The Community has been very conscious of the need to review its institutional arrangements and has published a number of reports which analyse the strengths and weaknesses of the institutions. The Report of the Vedel Group on the problem of increased powers for the European Parliament in 1972 provided a classic analysis of the workings of the institutions at that time and the report by the Belgian Prime Minister Leo Tindemans on European union in 1975 outlined, amongst other things, the institutional requirements for such union. In 1978 the European Council invited three experts to consider what was needed to adapt the institutions to carry out their existing functions and to progress further towards unity. The experts were Barend Bisheuvel, former Prime Minister of the Netherlands, Edmund Dell, former UK Secretary of State for Trade, and Robert Marjolin, former Vice-President of the European Commission. Their report, published in 1979, became known as the report of 'the three wise men'. In the same year the Commission appointed a review body under the chairmanship of former Dutch Ambassador Dirk Spierenburg to examine and make recommendations on the organisation and staffing of the Commission in view of the prospective enlargement of the Community to include Greece, Spain and Portugal.

Underlying the idea of an economic community is that of the political goal of greater peace and unity in Europe. This is clearly expressed in Article 2 of the Treaty of Rome which sets out the objectives of the Community. These are: harmonious development of economic activities; continuous and balanced expansion; increased stability; accelerated raising of living standards; closer relations between member states.

These aims are to be achieved by:
- establishing a common market for industrial and agricultural goods and a common external tariff on goods from third (non-member) countries
- the abolition of restrictions on the movements between member states of persons, services and capital
- the adoption of common policies on agriculture, transport and procedures to ensure competition in markets
- the approximation of the laws of member states to ensure a common market
- the progressive approximation of economic policies of member states
- the creation of a social fund to improve conditions for workers and of a regional policy to ensure balanced expansion
- association agreements with third countries.

A COMMON MARKET

A unified market in industrial and agricultural goods is so fundamental to the success of the Community that the Community itself is sometimes known simply as the 'Common Market'.

The objective is to create conditions for economic activity which approximate to perfect competition. Such conditions, economists argue, make industry and agriculture more efficient and raise living standards. The originators of the EEC ideal were deeply influenced by the example of the United States, which by exploiting the advantages of its own common market had become the world's dominant economy.

The first step in building a common market was the creation of a customs union, defined as a free trade area with a common external tariff. The member states gradually removed tariffs on each other's goods while the external tariff ensured that no member country gained a competitive advantage over another by, for example, being able to buy cheaper raw materials.

ABOLITION OF RESTRICTIONS

The corollary to the removal of tariff barriers to free trade is the removal of other restrictions on factors of production which distort trade and limit competition. Chief among these restrictions are limitations on the mobility of labour, capital, enterprise and services. The Treaty makes provision for the free movement of workers, business personnel, professionals and capital from one member state to another but the Community's success in implementing these provisions has varied. Manual workers have benefited most. It is now illegal to refuse to employ a worker from another member state on grounds of his or her nationality, except for public service jobs. Insured workers keep their entitlements to social security no matter where they live in the Community. The Community has also passed legislation to set standards for wages and working conditions which has significantly affected the employment of women. Some professional groups, such as doctors, dentists and midwives, have been given the right to offer their services in any member state but many others remain bound by national rules which discriminate against citizens of other member states.

Business personnel and craft workers have not yet been given the right to establish themselves in another Community country but the Court of Justice has ruled that member states may not discriminate in their laws or administrative practices against a national of another member state who wishes to set up a business. Considerable progress was made to allow capital to move freely in the Community but the recession of the past decade led some member states, including Ireland, to tighten exchange controls.

COMMON POLICIES

A common market needs agreed policies to guarantee market unity and competition. The Treaty provides a framework for common policies in transport and agriculture whilst maintaining competition and balance between regions. Progress towards a full transport policy, aimed at removing distortions in trade between member states because of different rules on the transport of goods, has been slow. The competition policy ensures that firms do not take unfair advantage of their position in the market to create monopolies or fix prices unfairly. The common agricultural policy, the most important policy of the Community, was designed to guarantee farmers a secure income and consumers an efficient supply of food.

APPROXIMATION OF LAWS

The Community's efforts to standardise the size of eggs, the system of weights and measures, the ingredients of beer and the definition of 'ice cream' led to protests and cries of 'bureaucracy', but there is a logic in such activities. There are many barriers to free trade because of the laws of member states or the absence of agreed standards. Belgium, for example has refused to allow margarine to be sold within its borders unless it is sold in square packets thus using a technicality to discriminate against margarine produced in different shapes by other member states. Agreement on the size of eggs permits much greater trade between member states and better protection for the consumer. A common metric system makes life easier for manufacturers because components of products, for example cars, will all be made to standard sizes. The harmonisation of laws relating to the manufacture and sale of goods follows from the creation of a common market.

APPROXIMATION OF ECONOMIC POLICIES

The Treaty envisaged that the Community would progress beyond a common market to economic union through the adoption of an agreed economic policy but it was vague about when and how this was to be achieved. The 1972 decision by the heads of government to establish an economic and monetary union by 1980 failed spectacularly. This union would have committed member states to restoring fixed but variable currency exchange rates within the Community to resolve the problems caused by the monetary instability of the early 1970s. The recession after 1974 dampened the enthusiasm of the members for the discipline involved. A major step, however, was taken in 1979 when eight of the nine partners, including Ireland, agreed to a European monetary system which has brought comparative stability to those currencies involved. Britain and Greece remain outside the system.

THE SOCIAL FUND AND REGIONAL POLICY

It was anticipated in the 1950s that under common market conditions some businesses would close, others would be restructured and new enterprises would be formed. Workers would be made redundant and unless they were retrained for a new job, would be unemployable. The purpose of the social fund, set up in 1958, was to help workers to change jobs or to move from one part of the Community to another. The scope of the fund has been widened over the years. It provides assistance when Community policies reduce jobs in a sector, helps women, young people or migrant workers find jobs, trains mentally and physically handicapped persons for employment and has supported a number of pilot schemes to combat poverty. In recent years, the social fund has been geared towards combating unemployment, particularly among young people.

The Treaty recognised that the less favoured regions of the Community would need special attention if they were not to lose out further in the common market. But it was not until 1975 that the partners agreed to the size of a special regional development fund. This fund provides additional aid to governments in carrying out their own regional policies, the bulk of its money being allocated on the basis of national quotas.

By volume of imports and exports, the Community is the world's largest trading power. It is not surprising then that it considers relations with the rest of the world important. More than a hundred countries have diplomatic links with the Community and it has commercial and cooperation agreements with over eighty developing countries. It has special or association agreements with other European countries such as Spain, Norway, Austria, Finland, Sweden, Switzerland, Turkey, which grant them favourable trading arrangements. Before joining the Community in 1982, Greece's relations with the Nine were regulated by an association agreement.

The independence of Community institutions would not be of much practical use if the Community could do little. But it can do much more than other international organisations such as the Organisation for Economic Cooperation and Development (OECD) or the Council of Europe. The Community is concerned with the whole field of economic activity within and between member states and, because of the importance of economics, the Community affects the life of everyone in the member states.

This being said, there are important limitations on the capacity of the Community to act. Firstly, unlike a state, it is not fully competent to exercise legislative, executive and judicial powers. Scope for Community action is closely defined by the Treaty and the Community cannot act unless it is empowered to do so by the Treaty. Secondly, decision-making power still rests at national level. There is no question of the Community 'imposing' a solution or policy without at least the passive agreement of member states. If member states wish to act together on an issue not covered by the Treaty they must agree unanimously to do so.

The Community has the potential for full economic union between the member states, but the political will for this is lacking. It has been very successful in building a common market but has been reluctant to tackle the problems associated with increased economic integration, such as approximating economic and monetary policies or establishing far-reaching social and regional policies. The main reason for its success in the former areas is the detailed nature of the Treaty provisions and time scales, supported by high economic growth in the 1950s and 1960s. Similar conditions do not apply to progress towards economic union. The effects of the recession in the 1970s and early 1980s made it difficult to agree on what needed to be done at Community level and for national governments to take radical decisions.

The Treaty provides the Council of Ministers and the Commission with several legal powers or instruments for executing their legislative and executive functions. The particular instrument used depends on the extent of the application intended. The most important instruments are: regulations, decisions and directives. For the most part, the Treaty sets out which instrument is to be used in each area of Community activity.

Regulations These are extremely powerful legal instruments. Article 189 of the Treaty of Rome says: 'A regulation may have general application. It shall be binding in its entirety and directly applicable in all member states.' This means that regulations have the direct force of law in any member state. It does not need to be converted into domestic law or be ratified by the national parliament to take effect. A regulation has supremacy over domestic law. It is equivalent to an act of the Oireachtas in an Irish context. The reason why we required a referendum in Ireland to ratify membership of the European communities was because our constitution had to be amended to take account of the supremacy of Community legislation over domestic law. This supremacy of regulations has been contested before and upheld by the Court of Justice. Regulations also generate rights and obligations for everyone in the Community.

A regulation will be used when the Community wants to introduce a measure which is to apply generally, where the provisions are fairly straightforward and important enough to warrant superseding existing national law. Regulations are usually used in connection with the common agricultural, transport and commercial policies. Regulations are mainly issued by the Council, or by the Commission in the areas where it has been delegated executive powers, for example in the management of the common agricultural policy. Because regulations are addressed to the Community at large they must be published in the *Official Journal of the European Communities* before becoming law.

Decisions A decision is similar to a regulation in its legal effect, but it is used to achieve something which has a particular application. For example, if a country applied to take protective measures against dumping, the Community would act by issuing a decision. A decision is always addressed to a particular member state, private company or public body. Decisions do not have to be published in the *Official Journal*, but they usually are. The majority of decisions are issued by the Commission and this reflects their use as instruments for the detailed implementation of the Treaty. Decisions are also used to fill out the framework of regulations where necessary.

Directives These are somewhat different from the above two instruments.

Article 189 of the Treaty of Rome states: 'A directive is binding as to the result to be achieved upon each member state to which it is addressed, but shall leave to the national authorities the choice of formal methods'. A directive is used when the Community wants to achieve an end, but it is not necessary to be specific about how that end is to be achieved. Directives are addressed only to the governments of member states; they, therefore, never create obligations for individuals in a member state but they do create rights. For example, directives were used to introduce the right of doctors and nurses from member states to practise their profession in any other member state. Likewise, directives are used for the removal of technical barriers to trade.

The Commission, in its delegated sphere of activity can make its own regulations, decisions and directives. The significance of the Community's means of action is that its legal instruments do not merely regulate the relations of the member states to each other but they provide legal rights (and often obligations) for Community citizens.

The unique character of the Community's institutions and its broad field of action are complemented by powerful means of action. Community laws agreed in Brussels have supremacy over domestic law in a way that the rules and conventions of other international organisations do not. For this reason, membership involves a transfer of national sovereignty to the supranational level of the Community, in the interest of European integration. At the same time, the checks and balances of the institutions ensure that national interests are respected and accommodated wherever possible.

In the run up to the first direct elections to the European Parliament the satirical magazine, *Il Male*, carried a cartoon of two Italians sitting on a bench in Rome. 'Who are you voting for?' the one asked the other. 'I think I'll vote for France,' came the reply.

3
The European Council

EEC leaders take a walk during the European Council meeting in Stuttgart, June 1983.

SIR HAROLD WILSON, former British Prime Minister, in an article in *The Times*, recalled how in early September 1974 President Giscard d'Estaing of France telephoned EEC heads of government inviting them to attend a meeting in the Elysée Palace eight days later to discuss European integration. When the leaders arrived without either foreign ministers or officials they were ushered into the President's room where they sat - not around a conference table but in high-backed chairs arranged in the shape of a horse-shoe. Instead of discussing European integration they talked about the practical problem of unemployment, the President seeking the views of each leader in turn but pointedly not those of the President of the Commission, François Xavier Ortoli. So enjoyable was the conversation that they agreed that such 'fireside chats' should be held regularly.

The heads of government, accompanied by their foreign ministers, returned to Paris soon afterwards for a summit meeting and announced the birth of a new body, the European Council. Significantly, they were establishing an institution not provided for in the Treaty of Rome though regular summits had become a fact of life. The reason given for setting up the Council was the recognition by the leaders of the need to ensure progress and overall consistency in the activities of Community institutions and in the Community's foreign policy. The European Council would meet at least three times a year, or when the need arose. The leaders would be accompanied at such meetings only by their foreign ministers.

The formation of the European Council has proved to be the most important institutional development since the 1965 victory of General de Gaulle over the Hallstein Commission. It established a 'cabinet' at European level, firmly putting the direction of the Community in the hands of government leaders in a way not provided for in the treaties. According to Sir Harold the European Council quickly became the principal decision-making body of the EEC, inserting a new political dimension not envisaged by the founders of the Community. Other observers, however, feared that such an institution usurped the legal role of the Council of Ministers, that it downgraded in importance the Commission and the European Parliament and that it posed a threat to the rights of the small member states through the dominance in debate of the more powerful leaders.

The first European Council took place in Dublin Castle in March 1975 and was attended by nine European leaders, their foreign ministers and by Commissioners Ortoli and Wilhelm Haferkamp. Officials, who were kept outside the room, were dependent for information about what was being said on notes that were written hastily by foreign ministers and slipped out of the room to them. Meetings of officials were held elsewhere in the Castle to work out a communique. In the evening the heads of government dined separately from their foreign ministers in an effort to recapture the 'fireside' informality.

The two-day meeting produced agreement on a budget concession to Britain and it arranged for continued access of New Zealand cheese to the Community market. The spectacle, however, of Community leaders haggling over technical details was in sharp contrast to the Giscardian concept of statesmanship. 'Here we are talking about cheese and not a word has been said about unemployment and inflation', complained Chancellor Helmut Schmidt of West Germany.

Since this debut the convention has been for two meetings a year to be held in the countries holding the six-month presidency of the European communities, while the third meeting takes place in either Brussels or Luxembourg. A pattern has developed of opening with lunch followed by an afternoon working session beginning with a review of the economic and social situation in the Community, followed by other items of topical concern. In the evenings, while the heads of government meet for dinner, the foreign ministers prepare the communique, usually with the help of officials. Talks resume the following morning and the meeting concludes at midday when the president presents the communique at a news conference.

The four meetings following Dublin produced declarations on foreign policy, summoned discussions on unemployment between governments, unions and managers, conferred honorary European citizenship on Jean Monnet and fixed a date for the holding of the elections to the European Parliament. But these were insufficient achievements and at a gloomy meeting in The Hague in December 1976 President Giscard said he intended to circulate proposals for improving the procedures of the European Council.

In early February 1977 Giscard informed his colleagues that they were heading in the right direction. 'Sometimes we settled certain questions,' he wrote, 'which were decisive for our common future - Great Britain's accession renegotiation, election of the European Assembly by universal suffrage - questions which we are well aware could not have been settled in any other way. Sometimes we had exchanges of views, in an atmosphere of frankness and intimacy which no other setting could have permitted.' Looking to the future he identified three types of subject for European Council deliberation:

- The European leaders should exchange their views on questions of European and international interest in as free and as frank an atmosphere as possible, civil servants and written statements to be kept to a minimum;
- Europe's leaders should speak with a distinctive voice on world issues through declarations agreed by the European Council;
- Matters not agreed by the Council of Ministers should come before the European Council for settlement.

It took until April 1978 for Giscard's faith in the European Council to be shared by the public. Public approval came with the news of preparations for the establishment of a European monetary system, a scheme which dominated the European Councils of Copenhagen, Bremen, Brussels and Paris. With this achievement to its credit the European Council was described by French Foreign Minister François Poncet as 'the dynamo' of the Community. Further confirmation of the pre-eminent role of the European Council came in a report on the institutions published in October 1979 by the 'three wise men'. In their judgment the European Council had become 'indispensable in the overall operation of the Community'. It was proof of the Community's 'capacity for self renewal in difficult circumstances'.

The 'wise men' listed three functions for the European Council:
- To provide a forum for free and informal exchange of views between the heads of member states;
- To discuss matters of treaty competence, foreign policy and issues of mutual concern outside the scope of the Community;
- Perhaps most importantly, to generate fresh initiatives and get the Community moving. Here they detected scope for development, arguing that the European Council could best break through bureaucratic impasses and give political spontaneity in Community affairs. To do this, flexibility in procedures would be necessary.

The European Council has no permanent secretariat, its organisation falling to the country holding the six-monthly presidency of the Community. (Early in 1984 President Mitterrand of France expressed support for a permanent secretariat for the European Council.)

There was no direct contact between the European Council and the Parliament until Taoiseach Jack Lynch attended the first session of the directly elected European Parliament in July 1979 in Strasbourg. Since then the head of government holding the presidency has reported to the Parliament on the outcome of the previous European Council.

The European Council was allowed little time to rest on its laurels after the creation of the European monetary system, for, in June 1979, a new British Prime Minister, Margaret Thatcher, announced her intention of seeking cuts in Britain's budget contribution. Thatcher plunged two successive European Councils - in Dublin and Luxembourg - into acrimonious and unresolved debate over her refund demands. Angrily, the heads of government passed the problem to the foreign ministers to settle which they did on an ad hoc basis in May 1980. This demonstrated the limits of the European Council and was viewed as a triumph for the normal decision-making machinery of the Community.

Since then the European Council has been absorbed in the effort of trying to find a solution to the linked questions of budget expansion, reform of the common agricultural policy, the development of new policies and a permanent agreement with Britain on its budget contribution. Its failure so far to find the solution has exposed it to the paralysis that beset other institutions. So pronounced was the failure of the Athens and Brussels meetings that there was not even the usual bland communique. So high are the stakes that President Mitterrand, as President of the Community, intensified efforts to find a compromise by touring the capitals of member states. Success would redeem the European Council and ensure that the Community had a future.

4
Council of Ministers

A meeting of the Council of Agriculture Ministers under the presidency of Jim Gibbons.

VISITORS TO BRUSSELS are awe-struck by the star-shaped glass building that towers over a district known as the Berlaymont and which is now the headquarters of the European Commission. Less impressive - perhaps not even noticed by the visitor - is another large building a stone's throw away beside the busy Rue de la Loi. It is a building which is often more alive at night than during the day. For it is here in the Charlemagne building that meetings take place of the Council of Ministers. It is here that agriculture and fisheries ministers engage in marathon sessions into the early hours of the morning, testing each other's physical and mental powers; it is here that foreign ministers discuss their approach to international crises; that finance ministers furtively devalue currencies or hatch plans for economic growth; that energy ministers devise schemes to reduce oil imports. The Charlemagne, in short, is where EEC governments take part in constant negotiation with one another. Late-night lights shining from the top floor of the Charlemagne are a sure sign that the Council of Ministers is again dead-locked.

For most of the year Council meetings take place in Brussels but in the months of April, June and October they are held in Luxembourg, in accordance with a long-standing agreement that shares institutions between the two capitals. At meetings of the Council in either Brussels or Luxembourg each minister speaks in his or her own language. Interpretation in the Community languages is simultaneous. Business is very slow. Ministers are accompanied by advisers; taking part also are commissioners and Council secretariat staff. Real debate is difficult to sustain as ministers tend to deliver prepared speeches. There is provision for ministers to go into restricted session, either alone or with only one official each, so that the politics of a compromise can be discussed more frankly. As meetings are held in private, the media are kept informed of developments through briefings from officials or from well-timed ministerial press conferences. Members of national parliaments are therefore largely dependent on media reports for knowledge of what takes place in the Council of Ministers. More often than not, Council meetings are indecisive: the large numbers attending the meetings inhibit decision-making.

The function of the Council of Ministers in the Community is to take decisions, pass laws and coordinate the economic policies of member states. There is one important limitation on its freedom to act; it cannot do so without a proposal for action from the Commission. A distinction is drawn between 'generalist' meetings of the Council and 'specialist' meetings. Generalist meetings are held when the foreign ministers meet to discuss questions relating to sources of revenue for the Community, trade, accession of new members and similar matters. Specialist meetings are meetings of ministers of agriculture, finance, industry and so on. The Council of Foreign Ministers has the further function of coordinating the specialist councils.

THE PRESIDENCY

The EEC presidency is taken by each of the member states at six monthly intervals, alphabetically according to their official names in their own language: Belgium, Germany, Greece, Denmark, France, Ireland, Italy, Luxembourg, the Netherlands and the United Kingdom.

The presidency convenes meetings of the Council and chairs those meetings. Good preparation and good chairmanship are essential ingredients for success. The president also organises meetings of the European Council and the follow-up to any decisions taken. The president is also responsible for the coordination of all meetings of the Council and of the working parties attached to it to ensure that the work of the institution forms a coherent whole. The president also has responsibility for providing the secretariat for meetings.

The president of the Council of Foreign Ministers plays an important role in dealings with other institutions and in the Community's relations with the outside world. In 1974 the Council agreed that there should be periodic contact between the president of the Council of Ministers, the Commission and the Parliament and that the incoming president should present a work programme for the six months ahead.

To date Ireland has held the Council presidency twice, in the first half of 1975 and the second half of 1979, and holds the presidency for a third time in the second half of 1984. The first Irish presidency, under the coalition government of Liam Cosgrave, was widely praised for its efficiency and its genuine search for Community solutions. Much of this was due to Garret FitzGerald who as Foreign Minister was an enthusiastic and energetic chairman. For instance, he began the practice of reporting the Council's activities to the European Parliament. The second presidency, under a Fianna Fáil government, was less distinguished, suffering from the disarray caused by the resignation as Taoiseach of Jack Lynch and the consequent attention of ministers to domestic rather than to EEC matters.

The workload of the presidency for a small member state involves a high number of officials relative to the size of the rest of the government machinery. That workload can be gauged from some figures relating to the first Irish presidency. During the first six months of 1975 Irish ministers chaired twenty-seven meetings of the Council in its various formations and Ireland provided the chair for some 190 Council committees and working groups. Under the framework of political cooperation Irish representatives played an active part in arranging and chairing meetings to coordinate the positions of the member states before and during the meetings of international organisations such as the United Nations, the Organisation for Economic Cooperation and Development and the Economic Commission for Europe. Irish representatives in non-member countries also chaired meetings of diplomatic representatives to discuss European political cooperation, matters of information and trade, and commercial and economic affairs.

Most member states want to have a good presidency but often, despite a strong motivation to succeed, presidents fail to resolve long-standing national differences. Weak presidencies may arise because objectives have not been clarified in advance and because of a lack of coordination between the different Councils, between working groups and even within the member state itself. An incoming presidency defines its priorities with the Commission but if it wavers in its commitment to achieving these it can hardly expect to provide clear leadership in Council. Psychologically, it is difficult for a small member state which usually does not carry much weight to be dominant when holding the presidency. The reality is that no presidency, big or small, can impose a programme nor define a course of action for the other partners. A good presidency may be the product of luck - that decisions were imperative; a bad presidency may be the victim of timing - that matters were not ripe for decisions. Whatever the circumstances, presidents, like athletes handing on a baton, try to ensure continuity in the main proposals requiring decisions.

VOTING

Unlike an inter-governmental conference, the Council can act by majority on matters not only of form but also of substance.

Article 148 of the Treaty lists three voting procedures for majority decisions. The most common is the 'qualified' majority where the Council acts on a proposal from the Commission. For an act to be passed, there must be at least forty-five votes cast in favour out of a total of sixty-three. Each country has a vote weighted according to its importance: Germany, France, Britain and Italy have ten votes each; Belgium, the Netherlands and Greece five each; Denmark and Ireland three each and Luxembourg two. Neither the big countries voting together (total forty votes) nor the small countries voting together (total forty-three votes) have enough to win a qualified majority. The 'big four' must have the support of at least one small country to carry the vote. The most important areas listed in the Treaty which require a qualified majority vote in the Council are the abolition of discrimination in regard to services, freedom of establishment and capital movement, the operation of the common agricultural policy and the transport and commercial policies.

The second kind of majority vote is taken when an act is not based on a Commission proposal. Again the minimum number of votes is also forty-five in favour, but these must represent the votes of at least six countries.

The least common form of majority voting is the 'simple' majority. This involves the assent of any six member states, the number of votes cast not being important. The Treaty says that this procedure should be followed where a form of voting is not specified. The 'simple majority' allows some national interests to be overruled in the interest of the majority of members and that is why it is used so seldom in Council.

In other cases, for instance Article 149, the Treaty requires the Council to take its decisions unanimously when it wants to amend a proposal from the Commission. This is to protect the interests of the Commission by making it difficult for the Council to change Commission proposals. In practice, drafts are often amended in Council by a compromise put by the president rather than the Commission. Article 148.3 states that abstentions do not prevent adoption by the Council of acts which require unanimity.

According to the Treaty the range of matters subject to majority voting was to be extended progressively, but the French boycott of Community institutions in 1965 thwarted this intention and led to the Luxembourg compromise which agreed not to use majority voting where a matter of vital importance to a member state was under discussion. Unanimity was to be sought instead. This was a setback for European integration, because decision-making became increasingly difficult. Qualified majority voting virtually disappeared from the Council.

If it was difficult to get six states to agree, the job was even tougher with nine. The enlargement of the Community therefore revived the arguments in favour of qualified majority voting. The 1974 Paris summit agreed that the possibility of majority voting should be considered in Council. In an attempt to do this Garret FitzGerald, as EEC President, tried to identify agenda items that fell within the Treaty category of majority voting. He asked member states at the start of a meeting to identify matters deemed to be of vital national importance. This isolated the issues for which unanimity could be obtained. This practice, however, did not last long.

On 18 May 1982 the Council of Agriculture Ministers defied Britain by taking a majority vote on the annual farm price increases. This was deplored by British Minister Peter Walker as 'a sad and damaging day in the Community's history' but it was played down as a 'one off' by Irish Minister Brian Lenihan who argued that Britain's objections were related to budget reform and not to the farm package itself and that Britain was unnecessarily holding up agreement. France and Italy entered into the minutes their belief that the adoption of the farm prices on the vote of seven member states did not amount to the ditching of the Luxembourg compromise. Greece and Denmark joined Britain in refusing to vote, thus supporting the unanimity system. The Commission backed the majority.

What happened was that the Luxembourg compromise was more rigorously defined on this occasion than previously. Until this event any member state could advance defence of national interest as the reason or pretext for blocking a Commission proposal. Rarely was a claim challenged even though there were frequent strains on the credibility of the term 'vital national interest'. Furthermore, the Luxembourg compromise intensified the wheeler-dealer nature of Council meetings. No longer were ministers seeking European solutions as their primary objective, they were bargaining for the maximum national benefit under the minimal European denominator. This gave rise to 'Euro-linkage' politics. In order to gain concessions on one front, member states would withhold consent on other unrelated issues. A consistent exponent of this was Britain, particularly in its manoeuvres on agriculture and the budget. The British opposed increased farm prices in order to win demands for a budget rebate. The Council, on a majority vote, passed the farm prices on the grounds that it was actually in the interest of British farmers to receive higher prices for their produce and that a vital national interest was not at stake. The principle of a vital national interest remained.

THE COMMITTEE OF PERMANENT REPRESENTATIVES (COREPER)

COREPER is one of the most important bodies in the EEC. It began on an informal basis in the early days of the EEC to facilitate the working of the Council, but gained full legal recognition in the 1965 Merger Treaty. It prepares the work of the Council of Ministers and carries out tasks the Council may assign it. The permanent representatives are special ambassadors accredited to the European communities, assisted by a staff of officials from the national ministries for foreign affairs and other ministries affected by Community activities. Their headquarters is in Brussels.

The Irish permanent representation consists of about fifty officials of whom twenty are of diplomatic rank. The range of expertise which they possess reflects the range of Community activities. Apart from officials from the Department of Foreign Affairs, there are officers from the Department of Finance, Agriculture, Fisheries and Forestry, Industry and Energy, Trade, Commerce and Tourism, Transport, Environment and Labour.

COREPER has two 'identities': the permanent representatives (COREPER II) meet two days a week to discuss the agenda of the 'generalist' foreign affairs Council while their deputies (COREPER I) meet to discuss the more technical subjects before the 'specialist' Councils.

To cope with the technical nature of most of its work, COREPER is assisted by over a hundred working groups. Some groups are very active and meet regularly, while others meet once or twice a year. Members of working groups are usually officials from the national administrations who travel to Brussels for meetings.

The chairmanship of COREPER follows the same rotation as the presidency of the Council. Its meetings, like the Council's, are held in camera, with Commission representatives attending. It has no power of its own to adopt binding acts, but its importance to the Community lies in its role of preparing Council sessions.

THE SPECIAL COMMITTEE ON AGRICULTURE

This committee, which was set up in 1960, prepares the meetings of the agriculture ministers. Its members are civil servants from the ministries of agriculture of the Ten. Its rules of procedure are the same as for COREPER and the Council.

Set up by a Council decision in 1974, this committee coordinates general economic policies, examines and compares member states' budgetary policies, prepares a preliminary medium-term economic policy programme and reviews the development of the economy of member states.

The political significance of the Special Committee on Agriculture, the Economic Policy Committee and especially COREPER stems from their role in preparing the Council of Ministers sessions. The bulk of Commission proposals passes through these committees and as many proposals as possible are agreed at this stage. Only the thorniest questions go on to be discussed at Council level.

The agenda of each meeting of the Council of Ministers is divided into two sections - the 'A' and 'B' sections. If agreement has been reached at COREPER level the subject appears on the 'A' list and the Council of Ministers has only to take a formal decision. This decision can be taken by any meeting of the Council, not necessarily a meeting of the ministers responsible. If COREPER cannot reach agreement, the matter comes under the 'B' heading and this means that it must be discussed in Council. In practice therefore, considerable decision-making powers devolve from the Council to COREPER and to the Special Committee on Agriculture and the Economic Policy Committee.

THE COUNCIL SECRETARIAT

The Council, COREPER and the working groups are assisted by the Council secretariat which writes the reports of the meetings of the Council, COREPER and working groups, and organises the press conferences for the president of the Council at the end of the meetings. It assists the chair in running the various meetings. The secretariat has built up a wealth of experience in procedures, personalities and subject matter. The short term of office of the presidents does not allow them to build up comparable expertise and they rely heavily on the advice of the secretariat particularly in resolving disputes between member states or breaking an impasse.

Much of the blame for the immobility in Community affairs is put on the Council. Indeed, the Council was subjected to critical assessment by the 'three wise men', who listed a number of failures. Firstly, agendas were overcrowded and badly organised with little distinction being made between major and minor items. Secondly, the Council's position as the main decision-making institution was being eroded, in an upward direction by the surrender of major decisions to the European Council and in a downward direction by inappropriate delegation of issues to civil servants. Thirdly, the role of the Foreign Affairs Council as the coordinator of the spectrum of Council business had been undermined by the poor attendance of foreign ministers at meetings. Fourthly, specialised meetings of the Council had multiplied without producing results or achieving an overall sense of direction.

Despite its weaknesses the Council manages to get through a fair amount of work. In 1983, for instance, it adopted forty-one directives, 395 regulations and 108 decisions, a substantial legislative feat if judged by the standards of the slow-moving Oireachtas.

One of the most unpleasant aspects of the disastrous EEC meeting of heads of government in Brussels in March 1984 was the dramatic deterioration in relations between the Taoiseach, Dr FitzGerald, and the British Prime Minister, Mrs Thatcher. The Taoiseach and the Iron Lady remained tight-lipped about the confrontation but the German delegation was not so reticent. A leading German newspaper, the *Suddeutsche Zeitung*, reported that at one point 'they nearly went for each other' as the summit became 'the forum for the drama of Irish partition going long back into history to the days of Cromwell'. *The Irish Times*, 24 March 1984

5
The Commission:
THE BARONS OF EUROPE?

A meeting of the European Commission with Commissioner Richard Burke in the foreground.

'THEY JET from place to place like millionaire playboys, dine sumptuously like baroque princes, spend their nights in the luxury of oil sheiks - and they pay not a penny out of their own pockets. The bills of the EEC commissioners are settled by the taxpayers . . . They manage the butter mountain and turn out regulations to harmonise tractor seats. But they also open frontiers and develop new markets.'

This extract from *Stern* magazine reflects the suspicion of the public that commissioners are 'barons of Europe' earning more than prime ministers, presidents and chancellors. While indulging this suspicion in the most ample tradition of popular journalism, the West German magazine article is based on a report from the Court of Auditors showing that in 1978 commissioners undertook 544 official journeys and were on the move 1,660 days, of which 517 were spent in their native countries.

The lifestyle of an EEC commissioner is in reality a lot less like a Dallas business tycoon than the above description suggests. Commissioners are not 'faceless Eurocrats'. They are senior Euro- civil servants and politicians, exercising economic and political powers under the Treaty. As well as formulating policies and implementing them, once decisions have been made by the Council of Ministers, commissioners have the task of explaining decisions to the public.

The Commission is the 'supranational' institution of the EEC designed to rise above national interest and to promote integration. To safeguard the independence of the Commission the Treaty states that it cannot be removed by the member states nor by the Council of Ministers but only by a vote of the European Parliament. The fourteen commissioners are, however, appointed by their governments, for a four-year period. Each of the bigger states - France, West Germany, Britain and Italy - nominates two commissioners, while the smaller states nominate one each. The Treaty lays down that the commissioners should be chosen for their 'general competence' and be persons whose 'independence is beyond doubt'. They are forbidden to take or seek instructions from any government, and governments undertake to respect this principle of independence. However, in recent years governments have not generally appointed their top people to the Commission. In recent years, too, the media, reflecting the stronger presence of national interest within the Commission, have tended to describe commissioners by nationality and pressure groups look to commissioners of their own nationality to fix things for them. In Ireland there is a widespread public misconception that our commissioner, more than government ministers, decides European policy as 'Mr. Europe'.

Commissions are known by the name of their president: Walter Hallstein, German, 1958-67; Jean Rey, Belgian, 1967-70; Franco Malfatti, Italian, 1970-72; Sicco Mansholt, Dutch, for a brief period in 1972 on the resignation of Malfatti; François Xavier Ortoli, French, 1973-76; Roy Jenkins, British, 1977-80; and Gaston Thorn, a Luxemburger, 1981-84.

Commission presidents are *primus inter pares*, lacking the authority that prime ministers enjoy in a national cabinet. To strengthen the president's role the 1975 Tindemans Report proposed that a·president be appointed before the other commissioners in order to influence the choice of colleagues and the allocation of jobs. Similarly, Taoiseach Liam Cosgrave, in a memorandum to the Rome European Council in December 1975, outlined a procedure for strengthening the independence of the Commission. 'Member Governments would first agree by common accord on a President-designate for the Commission: he would propose the other members of the Commission: the Parliament would be invited to approve the proposed membership, with a view to reaching common accord on appointment of those concerned, only after the Assembly had given its approval.' There was progress in the case of Roy Jenkins who was chosen in advance in 1976 as president, but he was, however, allowed little say in the choice of his colleagues. Matters receded in the case of Gaston Thorn when the European Council in Venice in June 1980 failed to reach agreement on his candidature. Both Thorn and Jenkins endured 'nights of the long knives', during which commissioners haggled over portfolios.

Each commissioner is assigned a portfolio which gives responsibility in a particular area, but decisions are made on a collegial basis by all commissioners. The Spierenburg Report has recommended that the number of commissioners be reduced to one from each country as there is insufficient work for the present fourteen.

MEMBERS OF THE EUROPEAN COMMISSION 1981-84 AND THEIR RESPONSIBILITIES

G. Thorn (President): secretariat general, legal service, spokesman's group, security office, cultural affairs.

FH.J.J. Andriessen: relations with the European Parliament, competition.

E. Pisani: development aid.

G. Contogeorgis: transport, fisheries, coordination of questions relating to tourism.

P. Dalsager: agriculture.

E. Davignon: industrial affairs, energy, Euratom Supply Agency, research and science.

A. Giolitti: regional policy, coordination of Community funds.

W. Haferkamp: external relations, including nuclear affairs.

K. H. Narjes: internal market and industrial innovation, customs union, environment, consumer protection, nuclear safety.

L. Natali (Vice-President): Mediterranean policy, enlargement, information.

R. Burke (replaced M. O'Kennedy in 1982): president's delegate, personnel and administration, joint interpreting and conference service, statistical office, publications office.

F. X. Ortoli (Vice-President): economic and financial affairs, credit and investments.

I. S. Richard: employment and social affairs, tripartite conference, education and professional training.

C. S. Tugendhat (Vice-President): budget and financial control, financial institutions, fiscal policy.

THE REMOVAL OF THE COMMISSION AND COMMISSIONERS

A commissioner once appointed cannot be removed from office by member states. If the Commission or the Council of Ministers is not satisfied that a commissioner is respecting the obligations of office, it can apply to the Court of Justice to have him or her removed. In July 1976 Albert Borschette was retired as a member of the Commission by the Court of Justice on the grounds that his state of health was preventing him from performing his duties as Commissioner for Competition, Personnel and Administration. A commissioner may also decide to resign. Michael O'Kennedy resigned following his election as a TD in the general election of February 1982. The Commission as a body is ultimately subject to the political control of the European Parliament. Parliament can compel the Commission to resign (but not individual commissioners) by passing a motion of censure. This power of Parliament is circumscribed by special conditions, the most significant of which require the motion to be passed by a two-thirds majority of the votes cast and a majority of Parliament's members.

The weakness of this weapon lies in the very strength it gives Parliament. The vote of censure is just too strong to use and it has never been used with success. In any case, if Parliament did force the resignation of the Commission the national governments could directly reappoint the same people. The fact that censure is always a possibility, however, may make the Commission more receptive to the wishes of Parliament. Certainly relations between the two institutions have been amicable, although the Commission has not always acted consistently in its relations with Parliament.

ORGANISATION

Each commissioner is assisted by a team of experts who form what is known as a 'cabinet'. The members of the cabinet organise the programme of appointments, public engagements and speeches; they represent the commissioner at meetings of officials at which proposals are prepared for presentation at the weekly Commission meeting; they ensure he is well briefed on matters likely to be raised by colleagues in other policy areas; they help their commissioner administer his portfolio, engaging in trade-offs where appropriate with other cabinets.

The commissioners are collectively responsible for twenty-eight departments, known as directorate generals and for administrative offices through which the work of the Commission is carried out. These are:

Secretariat-General of the Commission
Legal Service
Statistical Office
Customs Union Service
Environment and Consumer Protection Service

DG 1 - External Relations
DG 2 - Economic and Financial Affairs
DG 3 - Internal Market and Industrial Affairs
DG 4 - Competition
DG 5 - Employment and Social Affairs
DG 6 - Agriculture
DG 7 - Transport
DG 8 - Development
DG 9 - Personnel and Administration
DG 10 - Spokesman's Group and Directorate-General for Information
DG 11 - Environmental, Consumer Protection and Nuclear Safety Development
DG 12 - Research, Science and Education
DG 13 - Information, Market and Innovation
DG 14 - Fisheries
DG 15 - Financial Institutions and Taxation
DG 16 - Regional Policy
DG 17 - Energy
DG 18 - Credit and Investments
DG 19 - Budgets
DG 20 - Financial Control
Statistical Office
Euratom Supply Agency
Security Office
Office for Official Publications of the European Communities.

The typical directorate general is headed by a director general and is composed of a number of directorates which contain several divisions, the smallest administrative unit. A head of division corresponds to a principal officer in the Irish civil service. Thus the structure of a directorate general in the Commission is as follows:

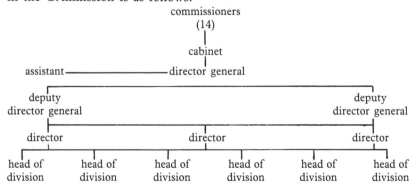

Article 155 of the Treaty defines the Commission's role as that of ensuring the proper functioning and development of the common market. Its most important power is the right to initiate policy proposals. The Council of Ministers cannot introduce a Community law unless it has received a proposal on the subject of such a law from the Commission. Article 21, for example, lays down that '. . . the Council shall, acting by a qualified majority *on a proposal* from the Commission, decide on any adjustment required in the interests of the internal consistency of the common customs tariff . . .' The Treaty also obliges the Council to seek the opinion or recommendation of the Commission, before opening negotiations on enlargement of the Community or tariff agreements with third countries.

The distinction between the Commission's right to propose and the Council's right to decide worked well in the early years of the Community but more recently it has not proved powerful enough to overcome the reluctance of member states to move towards greater integration.

Although the normal procedure in Community legislation is for the Council of Ministers to act on a proposal from the Commission, the Treaty permits the Commission to take some administrative decisions on the operation of the social fund and in the field of competition policy. The Commission is directed by the Treaty to maintain free competition by keeping cartels and monopolies within bounds, by regulating state subsidies and opposing discriminatory fiscal practices. The Commission also represents the Community in negotiations with non-member states and international organisations and in cases before the Court of Justice.

As the executive arm of the Community, the Commission has been delegated authority from the Council of Ministers to manage the common policies. Its most important responsibility is the common agricultural policy. To assist in its task of managing markets for agricultural products, the Commission has established management committees to advise it on proposals for each of the main group of products. Each committee consists of officials from the member states under the chairmanship of a Commission official. When a draft measure is submitted to a committee, each member expresses a national opinion, decisions being taken on a weighted vote system, as used in the Council. Unless there is a weighted majority against, the Commission is entitled to carry out its proposal. If there is a hostile vote, the matter may be referred to the Council - but this rarely happens.

The Commission was delegated administration of the European agricultural guidance and guarantee fund (FEOGA) in 1972 and of the regional fund in 1975. It also administers the European development fund and the joint research centres including the European Foundation for the

Improvement of Living and Working Conditions in Dublin. The Commission has the power to make laws - regulations, directives and decisions - without reference to the Council of Ministers in the areas where it has been delegated decision-making authority.

A vital part of the Commission's work is to ensure that community policies are put into practice in member states. In this role it acts as the watchdog of the Community. If a member state or a firm fails to carry out obligations under the treaties or Community legislation, the Commission first approaches the country or firm asking that the obligation be carried out, and requesting a reply within six weeks. If the complaint is not redressed, or if it is contested, the Commission issues a reasoned opinion, ordering observance of the law by a specified date. If that deadline is ignored, the Commission refers the matter to the Court of Justice in Luxembourg.

PERSONNEL

If its outer offices are included the Commission employs about 11,000 people, making it a far smaller organisation than is generally realised or the myth of Euro-bureaucracy entertains. The hard core in Brussels of about 8,300 is not excessively large, especially when compared with the 5,000 employees in Ireland's Department of Agriculture or the 7,000 plus in the revenue commissioners. It shrinks into insignificance against the 20,000 employees of the West German Ministry of Agriculture. One-third of the Commission staff is employed in the translation and interpretation service. The staff grading system is divided into five categories: A grades are policy makers equivalent to the top administrative grades in the national civil service and have university qualifications; B grades equate with executive grades and have second level educational qualifications; C grades are engaged in secretarial and clerical duties; D grades are involved in manual or service jobs (chauffeurs or doormen); the interpreters and translators form a separate administrative grouping with its own grading system.

In its recruitment policy the Commission attempts to keep a balance between nationalities, particularly at the more 'political' levels of director generals, directors and heads of division. In theory, no particular post can be reserved for any one nationality but in practice this is an important factor in job allocation. A disadvantage of working in the Commission is that promotion depends on nationality as much, if not more, than merit.

IRELAND AND THE COMMISSION

Ireland has professed to believe in the need for a strong and independent Commission. A good start was made with the appointment of Patrick Hillery, who, as Minister for Foreign Affairs, had negotiated Ireland's membership terms and had become a European figure. He secured a vice-presidency and was put in charge of the social affairs portfolio. From 1973-76 he succeeded in putting together the common social policy called for by the 1972 Paris summit. He also showed his independence by opposing the Irish government's attempt to evade the implementation of the equal pay directive for women. His successor Richard Burke, Minister of Education in the Cosgrave government, was subject to rude remarks about his 'rag bag' responsibilities but he surprised his critics by making full use of the transport, taxation and consumer platforms offered to him. High hopes were placed in Ireland's third commissioner, Michael O'Kennedy, who took over from Mr. Burke in 1981. As a former Finance and Foreign Minister - and a President of the Council - Mr. O'Kennedy seemed well placed to make his mark in the Commission. Mrs. Thatcher objected to his having a real say in the budget reform negotiations, and he found himself ill at ease in the vague role as assistant to President Thorn in these negotiations. He hankered for a return to Irish politics, a move which he made when a general election was held in February 1982.

To secure his minority Fianna Fáil government, Taoiseach Mr Haughey replaced O'Kennedy with former commissioner Richard Burke, a Fine Gael backbencher. The price for this overspill of domestic politics into Brussels was a lowering of the Irish image in the EEC. Burke inherited O'Kennedy's portfolio of personnel and administration, but he was given special tasks which he handled well, particularly the Greek Socialist government's renegotiation of its membership terms and Greenland's secession from the Community.

THE THORN COMMISSION

In 1981, the newly appointed President Gaston Thorn set his Commission the task of relaunching European integration but by the end of 1983, with the failure of the European Council in Athens, the crisis facing the Community which had been brewing for some time erupted. Thorn's priorities are reform of the common agricultural policy in order to save it from collapse and agreement on new budgetary arrangements. For the Commission a new phase of Community development means creating a European economic and industrial area to take advantage of the size of the Community market in the fight against unemployment and de-industrialisation, enlarging the EEC to include Spain and Portugal and giving the Community the resources it needs for further development. The Commission cannot achieve objectives without the support of the Council of Ministers, however.

'Without the Commission, the Community could never have been constructed. Without the Commission, the Community could not function even with the limited efficiency that it does today.' This verdict by the 'three wise men' in their report on EEC institutions is fair comment on a body which in the mid-1960s lost the battle for increased integration but which in the mid-1980s is trying to ward off the member states from the path of creeping disintegration.

The starting point of the analysis by the 'three wise men' of the situation in the Community is the shift in power away from the Commission to the national governments. Following the ill-fated clash with General de Gaulle, the Commission found itself dealing with governments which in the 1970s were on the defensive domestically against the twin evils of inflation and unemployment. 'This affected the Commission directly,' their report noted, 'in so far as States were less willing to heed its advice or to let it administer policies in the "European" interest. It also weakened indirectly the Commission's hold over the legislative process. A Council in which the States fought for narrowly national interests was not a place in which the Commission could easily mediate by appealing to the common ground.' In addition, the European Council has assumed political leadership in the Community. Yet, the 'wise men' believed that it was essential that the Commission should maintain an active role in the Community as it should stand for the interests of Europe as a whole.

Friday, 23 March 1984: Daisy, Anemone, Primrose and Prunella lumbered into an unemployment office in Tours, France, to claim benefits, maintaining that their jobs as milk producers had been taken away by new EEC milk production quotas. City officials dutifully opened files for the four dairy cows, described by the 250 farmers accompanying them as 'illiterate, single, working mothers with two to four dependents each'.

The Irish Times, Saturday, 24 March 1984

6
European Parliament:

RABBLE WITHOUT RESPONSIBILITY?

HAVING BEEN the most neglected of the EEC institutions the European Parliament now attracts greater attention as a result of the direct elections of June 1979 and 1984. As the only institution which is directly elected by the people - and the only one that meets in public - it is using its 'democratic legitimacy' to press for a greater say in EEC decision-making and for control over the budget. Yet, there is still disagreement as to whether this institution is a genuine Parliament or a mere talking-shop. It has aroused public cynicism, particularly in Ireland and Britain, for allegedly being a 'holiday camp' Parliament, the 'flying Parliament', the 'EEC gravy train', and, in the words of former Irish Foreign Minister Brian Lenihan, 'a rabble without responsibility'.

CHARACTERISTICS

The European Parliament consists of 434 politicians, fifteen of whom are from Ireland and three from Northern Ireland, elected for five years to represent 270 million citizens. It evolved from the common assembly of the 1952 European Coal and Steel Community. The Treaty of Rome in 1957 gave this assembly 'advisory and supervisory' powers in relation to the Commission and the Council. Officially called the European Assembly, it voted in 1962 to call itself the European Parliament. Until 1979 the members were nominated to it by the national parliaments. Today it monitors not only the work of the Commission and Council but also political cooperation and the European Council.

Unlike Dáil Eireann the European Parliament has no independent legislative functions nor do its members form a government. The Parliament has no say in the appointment of the Commission, nor of the Council. But unlike national parliaments where governments decide parliamentary priorities, the European Parliament fixes its own order of business. Its committee system is more highly developed than that of the Oireachtas. Practically every shade of European thought is represented - from communists to right-wing conservatives. And members are seated not by nationality but by political affiliation. Though they may have limited formal powers, the MEPs regard it as their democratic right to debate any subject of topical concern. In particular, they have taken strong stands on human rights questions.

The European Parliament lacks that fundamental ingredient essential to the character of parliamentary democracy - the struggle for political power among parties. There are no 'government' or 'opposition' parties in the European Parliament. Although the groups draw up policy guidelines and stand for distinctive political philosophies, they do not exert the tight grip employed by party whips in national governments. This can make for an apolitical atmosphere: you are unlikely to be trampled under a stampede of MEPs wishing to vote at the instigation of the party whip.

COMPOSITION

The first direct elections in 1979 resulted in an average turnout of 61% ranging from 92% in Belgium where voting is compulsory to 31% in Britain. Ireland, with a 63.6% turnout, was just above the EEC average. This average turnout - which though poor when judged by the standard of national elections in Europe was virtually as good as an American presidential election - returned a Parliament dominated by centre right groups of Christian Democrats (to which Fine Gael is allied), Liberals, British Conservatives and the European Progressive Democrats (the French Gaullist-Fianna Fáil partnership). The Socialists, among whom are the Irish Labour members, were returned as the largest single group.

The four biggest States, France, West Germany, Britain and Italy, each elect eighty-one members; the Netherlands twenty-five, Belgium twenty-four, Denmark sixteen, Ireland fifteen, (three Northern Ireland members are among Britain's eighty-one) and Luxembourg six. The total rose to 434 when Greece joined the Community in 1981 with twenty-four MEPs.

REMUNERATION

Initial proposals for the payment of MEPs were controversial. It was proposed to pay MEPs a salary above that of a West German parliamentarian. Although Irish deputies are poorly paid by European standards it did not seem just to pay Irish MEPs several times what their colleagues in the Dáil were earning. In December 1978 the European Council decided that MEPs would be paid on a national basis. An Irish MEP earns the same salary as a Dáil deputy (IR£16,413 in 1984) and is subject to national taxation. Deputies with a dual mandate - members of the Oireachtas and the European Parliament - receive both salaries. In early 1984 only about 11% of MEPs exercised the dual mandate.

There are also generous allowances for MEPs: a parliamentary overnight allowance of IR£87; almost IR£3,000 a month for an office and for secretarial/research assistance on the presentation of receipts; travel expenses are usually slightly more generous than the cost of air tickets and are especially profitable in the case of the direct Air France Dublin-London-Strasbourg flight which operates for plenary sessions on a half-price basis.

ORGANISATION

Elected as the Parliament's first president was a Liberal, Simone Veil, who had been Minister for Health in France. She was in the chair for the first half of the Parliament's five year term when she was succeeded by a Dutch Socialist, Pieter Dankert. The president, assisted by twelve vice-presidents - of whom one was Paddy Lalor, Fianna Fáil - organises parliamentary business in what is called the Bureau. This becomes the Enlarged Bureau when it is joined by the leaders of the political groups. It draws up the draft agenda for the week-long parliamentary sessions. Parliament meets each month except August but holds two plenary sessions in October.

Attending Bureau meetings in an advisory capacity are five questors, who have special responsibility for administrative matters. Like the president, vice-presidents and questors are elected for a term of 2½ years.

There is a staff secretariat, headed by a secretary-general and divided into five directorates general each under a director-general. These are: sessional and general services; committees and inter-parliamentary delegations; information and public relations; administration, personnel and finance; research and documentation. About two-thirds of the Parliament's staff are engaged in interpretation and translation work in the seven official Community languages.

A significant feature of the European Parliament is that its members are seated by political affiliation. The rules of procedure require that a political group shall consist of a minimum of twenty-one members provided they are all from the one member state, fifteen if they come from two states and ten if from over two states. A few members including the Rev. Ian Paisley are independents. But the advantages of belonging to a group are considerable in terms of financial and secretarial resources. The bigger the group, too, the bigger the influence it exerts in the internal business of Parliament, not least in securing time in debates and appointments to committees.

From left to right of the political spectrum there are six groups:

Communists and allies - 48 members

Socialists - 125 members

European Peoples' Party - 117 members
  (Christian Democrats)

European Progressive Democrats - 22 members

European Democrats - 63 members
  (Conservatives)

European Liberals and Democrats - 38 members.

There is also the pragmatic grouping known as The Group for Technical Coordination with eleven members, including Neil Blaney.

COMMITTEES

The plenary sessions of Parliament take up about sixty days a year, yet these sessions represent only a portion of Parliament's work. The bulk of its business takes place in nineteen committees which appoint rapporteurs to draw up reports on subjects for which an opinion is sought by the Council.

The committees are:

political affairs

agriculture

budgets

economic and monetary affairs

energy and research

external economic relations

legal affairs

social affairs and employment

regional policy and regional planning

transport

environment, public health and consumer protection

youth, culture, education, information and sport

development and cooperation
budgetary control
rules of procedure and petitions
verification of credentials
institutional affairs
status of women in Europe
toxic and dangerous substances.
Committee meetings are usually held in private but permission can be obtained from the Bureau to hold special public hearings - for example on consumer protection - at which interested groups and experts are allowed to present evidence to parliamentarians.

LOCATION

The location of Parliament is one of its major problems. Its official headquarters are in Luxembourg; the secretariat is disposed in Luxembourg and Brussels, but plenary Parliamentary sessions are held in Strasbourg. The cost of servicing Parliament, including the cost of transporting documents from one centre to the next, is high. Members suffer considerable inconvenience travelling to and from Strasbourg as it is not the most accessible of cities. Adding to Parliament's 'gypsy image' is the fact that committee meetings take place in Brussels, which though facilitating close contact between the committees and the Commission injects a further geographical complication to Parliament's work.

FUNCTIONS AND POWERS

The Budget   Under the Budget Treaties of 1970 and 1975 the most significant power of Parliament is its right to amend the draft budget and to reject it in toto. But if it does so spending continues at the previous year's rate on a month by month basis, known as 'provisional twelfths'. Only a few months after direct elections in 1979 the Parliament rejected the 1980 budget as a demonstration of its intention to acquire a greater say in the 'power of the purse' and in decision-making in the Community (for a description of the budget cycle see Chapter 9).

Advisory Powers   Article 137 of the Treaty of Rome says that the European Parliament 'shall exercise the advisory and supervisory powers which are conferred upon it by this Treaty'.

Parliament's advisory powers consist of giving 'opinions' on proposals when asked by the Council, but the Council is not bound to accept Parliament's opinion, though it cannot take a decision until it has received Parliament's opinion. Since 1973 the Council has agreed not to begin substantive consideration of Commission proposals until Parliament has provided its opinion. The presidents of the Council and of the Commission meet several times a year to discuss the action taken by the Council on the opinions of the Parliament.

When the Council sends a proposal to Parliament for its opinion, it is passed on to the relevant committee for investigation. The committee appoints a rapporteur who drafts a report for the benefit of the committee and when the committee has agreed the report it is referred to a plenary session of Parliament. It is the rapporteur who presents the committee's report to Parliament. The political groups will have discussed the report at their party meetings and they nominate spokespersons to suggest amendments or to support the report. Before the end of the debate the responsible commissioner or the president of the relevant council may address the Parliament. The debate concludes and a vote is taken. If the report is adopted, it is submitted to the Council as an opinion. If not, it goes back to the committee for further analysis.

In order to smooth out difficulties between the two institutions in the field of legislation the Council and Parliament have decided on a conciliation procedure, distinct from the procedures which exist for reconciliation on the Community budget.

Supervisory powers Parliament has significant powers of control over the Commission. The Commission is obliged to publish annually a general report on the activities of the Community which Parliament discusses in open session. Since 1970 the president of the Commission presents Parliament with a report on its activities and its programme for the year ahead. This allows Parliament the opportunity to comment on Community policies at their inception. The Commission takes considerable care to inform Parliament's committees of draft proposals which it is preparing and this allows Parliament to influence the shape of proposals before decisions are made. The close working relationship between Parliament's committees and the Commission allows for continued monitoring of Commission activity.

Since the establishment of the Court of Auditors the Parliament has acquired significant powers to call the other institutions to account for their expenditure under the budget. This function is known as the 'power of discharge'.

Parliament has the power to dismiss the Commission - but not individual commissioners - by a two-thirds majority of all members of Parliament. But the Council can reappoint the same Commission so that this power is limited. Four attempts to dismiss the Commission were made prior to 1979 - including a Fianna Fáil-French Gaullist motion - but all failed to win enough support. The first directly elected Parliament chose not to invoke this power, preferring to establish a good alliance with the Commission.

Parliamentary questions can be put by MEPs to the Commission and the Council on EEC policies, and also to foreign ministers on political cooperation and the European Council. Questions to the Council represent a small advance in communication between the Council and Parliament. As at a national level, the substance of parliamentary questions is not as important as the formality they demand. Written questions predominate in the European Parliament but commissioners and ministers do appear to answer oral questions and debates often follow. Since the advent of British and Irish members in Parliament, the parliamentary question has been used more frequently, perhaps reflecting the strong tradition of parliamentary questions at Westminster and Leinster House. However, there is evidence that the Commission does not react as promptly as it should to questions put to it by members. In 1978 out of 1,123 written questions only fifty-six were answered within the one month allowed. In 1983 Parliament tabled 1,946 written questions and put 926 oral questions.

Increased power Direct elections did not automatically give increased powers to the European Parliament, but as Roy Jenkins, former President of the Commission, said, the Parliament 'is bound to have more influence, to have increased authority and to have the opportunity to use its powers more effectively'.

European Council It is now common practice for the head of government of the country holding the presidency to address Parliament on the proceedings of the previous European Council. But suggestions that the president of the Parliament should attend European Councils have been ignored by governments.

IRELAND

Media reports of lavish expenses, junkets and of fold-up beds in the Strasbourg offices of MEPs made the Irish and British public suspicious of the Parliament. In Ireland's case doubts about the value of the Parliament were repeatedly aroused by seven replacements being made without by-elections in the Labour party's representation. As a result of complaints from the Parliament's Credentials Committee a European Assembly Elections Bill was introduced in the Dáil requiring a list of 'substitutes' to be on display in polling booths though not on the ballot paper.

A particular problem for Irish MEPs is the amount of time spent travelling to and from meetings, and, significantly, a Eurobarometer opinion poll showed that 73% of people questioned in Ireland said that their MEPs were 'too remote from the problems of the people who elected them'. Another difficulty is that national politicians tend to regard MEPs as second class representatives. Unlike a TD a Euro-deputy cannot deliver 'favours' or 'fix things' for constituents. An MEP's work is focussed on the lengthy process of drafting reports from a committee to plenary stage during which long hours may be spent lobbying on behalf of inserting an amendment promoting Irish interests - or in getting a section harmful to those interests deleted. One instance of this was the way Labour's Flor O'Mahony managed to obtain a budget credit for an urban development plan for Dublin. Generally, however, the Parliamentarians can canvass commissioners and ministers, adopt resolutions and make speeches - but they do not make the decisions.

Irish MEPs have concentrated on agricultural, regional and budgetary matters and have tended to ignore the questions of institutional reform, women's rights, international economic affairs and foreign policy, except when they detect a threat to Ireland's neutrality! Their record compares not unfavourably with other national groups. Former Ministers Richie Ryan and Paddy Lalor had the status and experience to run their groups with authority. Farming expertise abounded in former Agriculture Ministers Mark Clinton and Neil Blaney, in former IFA President T. J. Maher, and in Fianna Fáil's Noel Davern, while former Gaeltacht Minister Tom O'Donnell and former Minister for Lands Sean Flanagan, were active in voicing regional concerns. Irish members have the opportunity of taking a more professional approach to politics on account of the superior facilities provided by the European Parliament as compared with the Dáil and also because problems are viewed from an international perspective. Indeed, it can be argued that a term in Strasbourg is the equivalent experience for a young politician of being a junior minister.

PERFORMANCE

The first directly elected Parliament was critical of the institutional deficiencies in the Community and it pressed for a revision of common policies. Under the leadership of Italian Communist Altiero Spinelli a 'Crocodile Club' was formed as a pressure group. In July 1981 this group persuaded the Parliament to set up an Institutional Affairs Committee, selected from the political groups but without the participation of any Irish members. It appointed Mr. Spinelli as the coordinating rapporteur of an ambitious project to draft a European Union Treaty for ratification by the member states. This was adopted by the Parliament at the 1984 February session. Its main proposals include:
- Parliament would share with the Council of Ministers legislative and budgetary power and political control in the Union;
- Each government should have a minister who is specifically and permanently responsible for European affairs;
- The requirement of unanimity in Council would be abolished after a ten-year transitional period;

- In the joint exercise of decision-making by Parliament and Council either of them would forfeit its right to express an opinion on a proposal within an appointed time;
- The European Council would appoint the Commission president but he or she would be responsible for setting up the Commission which would take up office only if it received the endorsement of Parliament;
- The Court of Justice would have greater and wider powers in ensuring a uniform interpretation of the law;
- Budget: Parliament would not only have the final word on the budget but it would have a say in agricultural spending. The Union would be able to raise the VAT level of the Community's own resources above 1% without having to consult national parliaments, thus permitting an expansion of regional and social, industrial and energy, environmental and transport policies.

The 1979 elections brought many of the big names of European politics - Willy Brandt, Jacques Chirac, Georges Marchais and Gaston Thorn among them - to Strasbourg but their attachment to that Parliament was fleeting. The task of establishing more efficient procedures and of fighting for political recognition was left to what journalist John Healy described as 'the forgotten men and women'. Of the 434 members some have left a legacy: Pieter Dankert for his extension of the Parliament's budget powers; Altiero Spinelli for his blueprint for reform; John Hume for bringing Northern Ireland to the centre of Parliament's business, Pancratzio Pasquale for pushing a revised regional policy, Egon Klepsch and Niels Haagerup on security.

IRISH CONSTITUENCIES

The map shows the four Irish constituencies and the Northern Ireland constituency. Munster has five seats and Dublin four. Leinster and Connacht/Ulster are three-seaters, as is Northern Ireland.

7
The Court of Justice

The Court of Justice, Luxembourg.

THE COURT OF JUSTICE in Luxembourg plays a much greater role in the development of the Community than might at first be apparent. Its task is to ensure that the rule of law operates in the communities. With the establishment of the European Coal and Steel Community new rights and obligations were created at a Community level which national courts were ill-equipped to handle. There were gaps in the treaties and interpretations of certain questions differed.

Had disputes been left to national courts to settle, the interpretation of the law and the quality of legal redress would have varied greatly from state to state. There would have been little coherent development of Community law as such. When the EEC and Euratom Treaties were signed, the Court was given jurisdiction over those communities. The judges have interpreted their task creatively by handing down decisions which have removed deficiencies in the treaties and settled how particular provisions are to be interpreted.

The Court has laid down rules on how this new body of European law relates to the national legal systems of the Ten. Many cases have been brought before it which have challenged the legitimacy and scope of Community law: the Customs Union or the CAP, for example, brought about such profound changes in the existing markets of member states that it was only to be expected that disputes would arise. Decisions however have been based on the spirit and goals inspiring the treaties, namely, the achievement of greater integration of member states. The Court upheld the authority of Community institutions, especially that of the Commission. Through a procedure known as the preliminary ruling the Court has assisted national courts in developing a standard approach to and interpretation of Community legislation. In this way it has contributed to the increasing uniformity of the legal systems of the member states. In the last decade, the Court has acted as a bulwark against the nationalism and protectionism of member states as political and economic difficulties reduced their commitment to free competition and the discipline of the common market.

The Court cannot enforce its decisions by sending anyone to jail, but it can and does impose fines. While companies have readily accepted its decisions member states have been more reluctant to obey, particularly when the Court has ruled against them for failing to implement a directive.

ORGANISATION

The organisation of the Court is significantly different from that of the Irish courts. The form and procedure of the Court owes a good deal to the Conseil d'Etat, the supreme administrative law court of France. The judges are assisted in their deliberations by five advocates general, officials unknown in the Irish public legal system. The closest parallel in this country is the military court which uses advocates general in a role similar to that of the EEC Court.

While the Court may meet in plenary session with all the judges present, cases are usually decided by one of the three chambers into which the Court divides to get through the work before it. Direct actions before the Court open with written submissions from the parties to the action and these submissions are scrutinised by a judge who acts as rapporteur to the case. A public hearing follows where the parties argue their case before the judges. Following the continental legal tradition, judges intervene to question witnesses during the hearing to a degree unknown in Irish courts. Some weeks after the oral hearing, the advocate general appointed to the case makes a submission for the guidance of the Court in its judgment. The submission is a detailed examination of the facts of the case and of the relevant law, and includes a suggested decision. Having considered the submission, the judges come to their decision which may depart significantly from the suggested decision of the advocate general. Judgments are short and reserved, that is, they are not given immediately the case concludes. They are always majority judgments and no dissenting judgments are given. The average length of time between the initial pleadings and the Court's decision is eighteen months, which compares favourably with the time it takes to decide cases in the superior courts of member states. Each case is conducted in the language of the defendant. When the Irish government appears before the Court, its case is presented by a barrister instructed by the chief state solicitor. Irish firms and private individuals must instruct an advocate who is properly qualified to practise before an Irish court.

JURISDICTION

The jurisdiction of the Court is extremely wide: it has powers to hear cases which in the legal system of member states would be spread across a number of courts. It is at one and the same time a constitutional court, an administrative court, a federal court, an international court and a staff tribunal.

Constitutional The Court has the power of judicial review over Community legislation. It can declare a piece of Community legislation null and void because it conflicts with the provisions of the Treaty of Rome. The Court also has the power to consider whether international agreements entered into by the Community are in conformity with the treaties. In these respects, the Court resembles the Irish Supreme Court which has the power to review legislation in the light of the provisions of the constitution.

Administrative The Court is administrative insofar as it can declare Community laws and administrative acts illegal if they fail to conform to certain principles of law-making.

Federal Under Article 177, the Court may assist courts in member states in which cases involving points of Community law are being heard by giving an interpretation of the relevant law. This has proved most influential for the development of Community law.

International It settles disputes between member states under the treaties and between Community institutions and member states.

Tribunal The Court has a function in settling disputes between staff working in Community institutions and agencies and their employers.

A number of actions may be brought before the Court under the Treaty of Rome. In the first type a member state can be brought before the Court for failing to fulfil an obligation under the Treaty. The Commission or another member state may bring the action. The Commission has taken member states to court quite frequently (Table 1). Sometimes there is a deliberate intention by a member state to avoid an obligation, but in most cases it is a question of misinterpretation of legislation or of delay in giving it effect in the member state. Italy is often at fault because of the cumbersome nature of its legislative process which causes delay in implementing Community law.

Secondly, the Court has power to review the legality of acts, regulations, decisions and directives of the Council of Ministers and of the Commission. The Court is entitled to find an act illegal and to declare it void but is not entitled to replace it with an act of its own. The grounds on which an act may be declared illegal are:
- the Council or Commission had no competence to act
- the proper procedures were not followed, for example, the Council of Ministers failed to consult the Parliament as required by the Treaty of Rome
- the act is an infringement of the Treaty of Rome or any rule of law relating to its application
- the act is a misuse of power by the Commission or Council of Ministers.
These four criteria which are taken directly from French administrative law represent an important safeguard against illegal or unreasonable acts by the Community institutions.

The most common ground for annulment is that the act in question infringes existing Community law. The majority of such actions have been brought by member states against the Commission but in 1971 the Commission brought an unsuccessful action against the Council of Ministers under that heading.

Table 1

Actions Brought to Court of Justice Alleging Failure of Member State to Fulfil its Obligations, 1953-1980

	1953-76	1977	1978	1979	1980	1981
Belgium	5	1	2	4	8	9
Denmark	—	—	1	—	1	2
Germany	3	—	1	1	1	2
France	9	2	3	2	4	6
Ireland	—	1	—	1	1	3
Italy	24	3	5	7	11	19
Luxembourg	2	1	—	1	2	2
Netherlands	2	1	—	—	—	5
UK	—	1	3	2	—	2
Total	45	10	15	18	28	50

Source Synopsis of the work of the Court of Justice of the European Communities.

Natural and legal persons (individuals and companies) may also bring actions against acts of the Community. The act must be of direct concern to a person before they can challenge it in the Court. Individuals have brought successful actions but the Court demands very good evidence that the applicant is individually affected. It is almost impossible to test the legality of regulations, which are binding on a large number of persons. An individual must prove that it somehow affects him or her differently from other persons. Individual appeals against decisions stand a better chance, as decisions affect a smaller number of people.

The third type of action that may be brought is when the Commission or Council has *failed to act* in cases where the Treaty obliges them to act. Member states and other institutions may bring such an action. The action will be accepted by the Court only if there is a binding obligation stated in the Treaty that the Council or the Commission must act - the obligation to act must be more than discretionary. The institution must also have been called upon to act first. Individuals can bring an action only in cases where the Commission or Council has failed to address an act to that person after they have been called upon to do so.

There is one way in which an individual can indirectly attack the legality of a regulation: this action is called a plea of exception of illegality. This means that an individual may bring an action to annul a decision on the grounds that a regulation on which a decision is based is void on one of the four grounds previously mentioned. This is one of the less obvious ways in which the individual is protected under the Treaty of Rome. If this protection did not exist an individual would have no right of redress against a decision, legal in itself, but based on an illegal regulation.

Table 2

Workload of Court of Justice of the European Communities

	1973	1974	1975	1976	1977	1978	1979	1980	1981
Preliminary rulings	61	39	69	75	84	123	106	99	109
Direct actions	31	22	35	32	50	123	63	80	120
Staff cases	100	41	26	19	24	22	1163	116	93

Source Synopsis of the work of the Court of Justice of the European Communities.

ACTIVITIES

The Court has played a notable part in ensuring that member states and firms operating in the Community observe the principles and rules of the common market. It has taken a tough line with governments which have introduced duties, taxes or restrictions which discriminate against the manufacturers or traders of other member states. It has offered redress to manufacturers or traders who were the victims of unfair competition or of monopolies abusing their dominant position on the market. It maintained the momentum for the free movement of persons and equal pay for men and women when the enthusiasm of the member states in the Council of Ministers waned. While the common agricultural policy has many problems, the decisions of the Court have ensured that the complex mechanisms for managing markets have functioned with the minimum of legal loopholes.

THE PRELIMINARY RULING

The preliminary ruling is one of the most interesting aspects of the Court's work. This procedure is necessary in the Community because, in the ordinary way, Community law is enforced through national courts. The preliminary ruling provides the link between the EEC Court and the national court. When a point of EEC law arises in a national court in the first instance, the judge has discretion whether or not to ask the Luxembourg court for a ruling. A judge in a national court of appeal must ask for a ruling if requested to do so by one of the parties to the action. Under the Treaty, the Court can give preliminary rulings to national courts on the interpretation of the Treaty, the validity and interpretation of acts of the Community and the interpretation of the statutes of bodies established by an act of the Council of Ministers.

The ruling given by the Court is binding on the judge in the national court. The interpretation also serves as a precedent in subsequent cases but a judge is free to ask for a new interpretation if he thinks it necessary. When the national judge receives the ruling, the case resumes and he applies the interpretation of the EEC Court to the facts as he sees fit. By mid 1982, Irish courts had requested preliminary rulings on nine occasions.

The action brought by the Irish Creamery Milk Suppliers against the Irish Government's 2% levy on farm produce in October 1979 as being contrary to existing EEC law illustrates how the preliminary ruling works. The case was heard in the High Court and because points of EEC law were raised, the judge referred the case to Luxembourg for an interpretation of the relevant legislation. The Court of Justice advised the High Court in March 1981 that a levy on agricultural producers which was part of a national incomes policy was not incompatible in principle with the provisions of the Treaty or the common agricultural policy. Having specified the conditions under which such a levy might conflict with EEC law the Court of Justice left it to the discretion of the High Court to decide whether

66

in the case before it those conditions did or did not apply.

The preliminary ruling provides a means whereby Community law is increasingly integrated into the domestic law of member states and common principles of law are applied throughout the Community. If the procedure did not exist the High Court would have to decide on the interpretation of Community law. This would lead to differences of interpretation between member states. As the Court has put it: 'Article 177 (the preliminary ruling) is essential for the preservation of the Community character of law established by the Treaty and has the objective of ensuring that in all circumstances this law is the same in all states of the Community.' (Case 73/166 European Court reports.)

CHARACTERISTICS OF COMMUNITY LAW

Community law is a distinct body of law consisting of the treaties, amending instruments and the binding acts of the Community institutions - regulations, directives and decisions. The special characteristics of each of these binding acts have been discussed in chapter 2. The main characteristic of this body of European law is its supremacy over domestic law. The concept of the supremacy of Community law has been developed to elucidate the relationship between Community law and the domestic law of each member state. The main implication of this concept is that in a case of conflict between Community and domestic law, Community law takes precedence. The main arguments used by the Court in its judgments upholding the supremacy of Community law are that:
- the member states have limited their sovereign rights and restricted their competence in certain fields and have transferred power to the Community
- the Community is a new legal order which creates rights and obligations not only for states but also for individuals
- to achieve the aims of the Community the law must be applied uniformly in all member states and, to ensure this, it must supersede domestic law.

Although the Court of Justice affirms the supremacy of Community law, the member states do not wholeheartedly agree. The reception given to Community law varies from state to state, depending on the constitution and legislation in each country. The original six members have essentially accepted the idea, though with different degrees of clarity. The concept poses no problem in principle for Irish law. The constitution, as amended by the EEC referendum in 1972, recognises the supremacy of Community law. In Britain the situation is more ambiguous because of the theory that parliament is the supreme law-making body in the state and that no parliament is bound by the acts of a previous parliament.

Despite Ireland's recognition of the supremacy of Community law, problems have arisen about giving this supremacy practical effect. In 1979 the Commission brought Ireland before the Court for failing to fulfil its obligations under Article 95 of the EEC Treaty. The complaint arose because the Irish government permitted home manufacturers of spirits, beer and made wine to defer payment of excise duties but charged imported spirits, beers and made wines excise duty at the date of importation. The Court rejected the defence put forward by the government and found that Ireland had failed to fulfil its obligations under the Article by giving a preferential benefit to Irish producers. The effect of the decision was to render the Imposition of Duties Order, 1975, under which the discriminatory duties were levied, null and void and the government was obliged to refrain from discriminating between home and Community producers.

In 1982 the Commission brought the government before the Court again on the grounds that the 'Buy Irish' campaign conflicted with the country's obligations under the Treaty. The Court found that the government-sponsored campaign, by encouraging the sale of Irish products at the expense of products from other member states, was in conflict with Article 30 of the Treaty. As a result of this decision the government can no longer fund a 'Buy Irish' campaign in Ireland. A campaign can, however, be carried out on a voluntary basis by Irish manufacturers. The Court's decision does not prevent the government from sponsoring Irish sales promotions in other member states.

The supremacy of Community law is ensured in practice through the operation of two concepts of law, known as 'direct effect' and 'direct applicability', which concern the status which Community law enjoys in the domestic legal systems of the member states. Direct effect refers to the extent to which individuals can invoke Community legislation against a member state - in other words whether the legislation confers on them *rights* which the domestic courts have to uphold. Direct applicability includes direct effect but is a wider concept referring to the extent to which Community legislation imposes *obligations* on the member state, companies or individuals to whom the legislation is addressed. In practice this means that the addressee cannot hide behind existing domestic law or the lack of it to evade an obligation to act under Community legislation.

The concept of direct effect has been developed by the Courts in its judgments. The Court has laid down that regulations always have direct effect. Treaty provisions and provisions of directives, decisions and of international agreements, provided they are clear and unconditional in what they propose, are also considered by the Court to have direct effect.

The concept of direct applicability is mentioned in the Treaty of Rome (Article 189). It applies to all regulations and to decisions addressed to individuals. Directives or decisions addressed to a member state do not create obligations for individuals; these obligations can be created only by the implementing legislation used by that member state. An example will illustrate the difference between two concepts. In 1977 the Community issued a directive to all member states requiring them to adjust their domestic legislation and procedures to allow for the free movement of doctors within a certain period of time. From the time this directive became law at Community level it gave *rights* (direct effect) to doctors in member states. If, for example, a member state did not fulfil its obligations within the set time, a doctor could bring a case against the member state in a national court. However, it was not until the domestic implementing legislation was put in force that doctors, hospitals, medical teaching centres, registration and other relevant bodies were *obliged* to play their part in ensuring the free movement of doctors (direct applicability).

The operation of direct effect and direct applicability gives Community law an unique standing as a legal system.

GENERAL PRINCIPLES OF LAW

Although the Court of Justice is mainly concerned with interpreting the written sources of law of the Community, it does use general principles of law to supplement the written texts. Such principles include non-retroactivity of legislation, respect for acquired rights, the notion that administrative bodies must act reasonably, the right of a person whose interests are affected by the decision of a public body to be given an opportunity to put a case. Many of these notions have found their way from national legal systems to the Court of Justice. Recently the Court has referred to the fundamental rights of citizens in cases coming before it. Such rights were invoked in the Utili case where the Court considered the extent to which a member state (France) could restrict the right of a national of another member state (Italy) to live in France. (Case 75/36 European Court reports.) In this case the Court made specific reference to the Council of Europe Convention on Human Rights without saying it was part of Community law. Significantly, in April 1977, the Parliament, the Council of Ministers and the Commission adopted a joint declaration in which all three institutions recognised the importance of the fundamental rights of citizens under the constitution of member states and the Convention on Human Rights and guaranteed to respect and continue to respect these rights in carrying out their functions under the Treaties. This shows that the legal system of the Community does not operate in a vacuum. It draws when necessary on principles of domestic and international law to assist it in its task of ensuring that within the Community the rule of law is observed.

8
How Decisions Are Made

There are many different ways of influencing EEC decisions!

THE DAY-TO-DAY WORKING of the Community consists of constant negotiation. The search for agreements acceptable to all member states requires a decision-making system that is sophisticated - but is also cumbersome and slow. Using a hypothetical example - the right of architects to practise their profession in other member states - this chapter describes how decisions are made in the Community.

The Community has power to act on the question of architects under provisions of the Treaty governing the free movement of persons and services. Article 57 reads:

> In order to make it easier for persons to take up and pursue activities as self-employed persons, the Council shall, on a proposal from the Commission and after consulting the Assembly (Parliament), acting . . . by a qualified majority . . . issue directives for the mutual

recognition of diplomas, certificates and other evidence of formal qualifications.

Article 63 gives the Community power to outlaw restrictions on the freedom of professional people to provide services in member states other than their own. The procedure laid down is the same as under Article 57 with the additional proviso that the Economic and Social Committee (ESC) be consulted.

While a member state may not introduce any new restrictions to limit the right of self-employed or professional people from other member states to establish themselves or provide services in its territory, the Treaty did not commit the partners to a specific date for allowing free movement of persons and services. The Community began many years ago to explore the possibility of mutual recognition of architects' diplomas but little was achieved.

INITIATION

The initiative would be taken by the Commission after lobbying by interests such as a member state, the Parliament, the Economic and Social Committee or groups representing architects and the building industry. The Commission would then make a proposal covering three main issues: the mutual recognition of architectural qualifications, removal of any discrimination on the employment of nationals from other member states in architectural firms and the granting of equal rights to architects from other member states to set up in business in the country of their choice. A number of problems would have to be overcome. The length of training varies from state to state and architects are not qualified to do the same things in all member states. There is the question of whether the allied professions of architectural draughtsman and technician should be given the same privileges as architects and the issue of equal recognition of university and technical college degrees. A small member state like Ireland might feel that its architects would be threatened if large firms from the bigger member states were given the right to set up in business within its borders. Interested parties are given early and complete notice of the Commission's intentions in the annual 'action programme' in which the commissioners publicly announce the policies they will pursue.

PREPARATION

The initial preparation takes place in the smallest of the Commission's administrative units - the Division. A proposal on architects would be prepared by a Division of Directorate General 3 Internal Markets (DG 3). The first draft of the proposal is drawn up in consultation with relevant interests, both at a European level and in member countries. The Commission in this case would discuss its ideas with the two bodies representing architects at Community level - the Liaison Committee of the Architects of Europe and the European Committee of Landscape Architects. The Commission would consult the government agencies with general responsibility for the education and recognition of architects and the organisation of the construction industry. In Ireland this would include the Departments of Education, the Environment, Industry and the Higher Education Authority. It would also meet representatives of the governing body of the profession in each member state, such as the Royal Institute of Architects in Ireland.

In its preliminary consultations the Commission tries to reach a broad level of agreement among all the interests. Since the Council reaches its decisions unanimously and not by majority vote as required by the Treaty, the Commission is obliged to reach a common denominator of agreement between member states before submitting its proposal to the Council. During this preparatory stage, Parliament, through its Economic and Monetary Affairs Committee, is kept informed by the Commission on an informal basis of the progress of a proposal.

When DG3 secures sufficient agreement from interested bodies, it finalises the draft proposal and circulates it to other DGs which might be affected. It is examined by the Legal Service of the Commission to check that the proposed measure is consistent with the Treaty and existing Community law and that the presentation follows the rules which the institutions traditionally observe in drafting legislation. The proposal is then presented by the commissioner for DG3 for decision by fellow commissioners.

A COMMISSION PROPOSAL

The Commission takes decisions by a majority of its members. It does so either by written procedure or after discussion. Under the more commonly used written procedure, the text of the draft proposal is sent to each commissioner with a note that if no objections have been lodged within a given time, the proposal will be deemed approved. The time limit depends on the urgency of the proposal; if it is not urgent, the limit is five days. An urgent proposal is dealt with immediately. If an objection is raised, the proposal must be discussed by the commissioners at one of their meetings, held at least once a week. They hold special meetings on particularly important or complex issues. Three senior officials of the Commission may attend these meetings - the secretary general, the director general of the legal service and the spokesman (press officer). Since the free movement of architects is an important proposal, it is likely that objections would be raised by other commissioners and the matter placed on the agenda of a commission meeting.

The Commission's meetings are prepared in advance by the chefs de cabinet (heads of the private offices of the commissioners) and chaired by the secretary general of the Commission. The chefs cannot take final decisions on proposals but they simplify decision-making for the commissioners. They agree on many technical points and the Commission has only to formally adopt their recommendations. Where agreement is not reached, differences may be narrowed and the objections of commissioners are at least clarified. Officials from the Legal Service, the Spokesman's Office and the relevant DGs may attend to assist the chefs in their discussions. If the chefs fail to agree the proposal is discussed by the commissioners and amended to the satisfaction of the majority. A formal 'proposal' of the Commission is born. It is usually published at this stage and forwarded to the Council of Ministers to be enacted as a directive.

THE COUNCIL CONSULTS

Under Articles 57 and 63 of the Treaty, the Council is obliged to formally consult the Parliament and the ESC. Parliament's opinion is prepared in the Economic and Monetary Affairs Committee, a member of which is appointed rapporteur to prepare a draft report for discussion. The Committee meets regularly and the Commissioner responsible for the proposal, or at least a senior official from the DG, attends. Representatives of the Council secretariat, COREPER and outside experts may also be asked to attend. When the Committee agrees on the report it submits it as a draft resolution to be passed by the Parliament in plenary session. The resolution sets out in detail how the Parliament thinks the proposal should be amended. Once agreed, this becomes an opinion of the Parliament and is formally dispatched to the Council. Conscious of the need for an ally in the face of the more powerful Council, the Commission takes the views of Parliament very seriously and tries to revise its proposal to the Council to accommodate the recommendations made in the opinion. In formulating its opinion, the ESC follows a procedure similar to that of Parliament.

COREPER AND THE WORKING PARTY

The Council is not in a position to engage in detailed discussion of Commission proposals. This task is delegated to COREPER. While the Parliament and the ESC are preparing their opinions, COREPER sets up a working party composed of experts on the subject from all the member states, usually civil servants from the relevant ministries. The working party attempts to reach agreement on the proposal and may hold many meetings over a long period. Commission officials attend and contribute

Diagram 1 - DECISION MAKING IN THE EEC

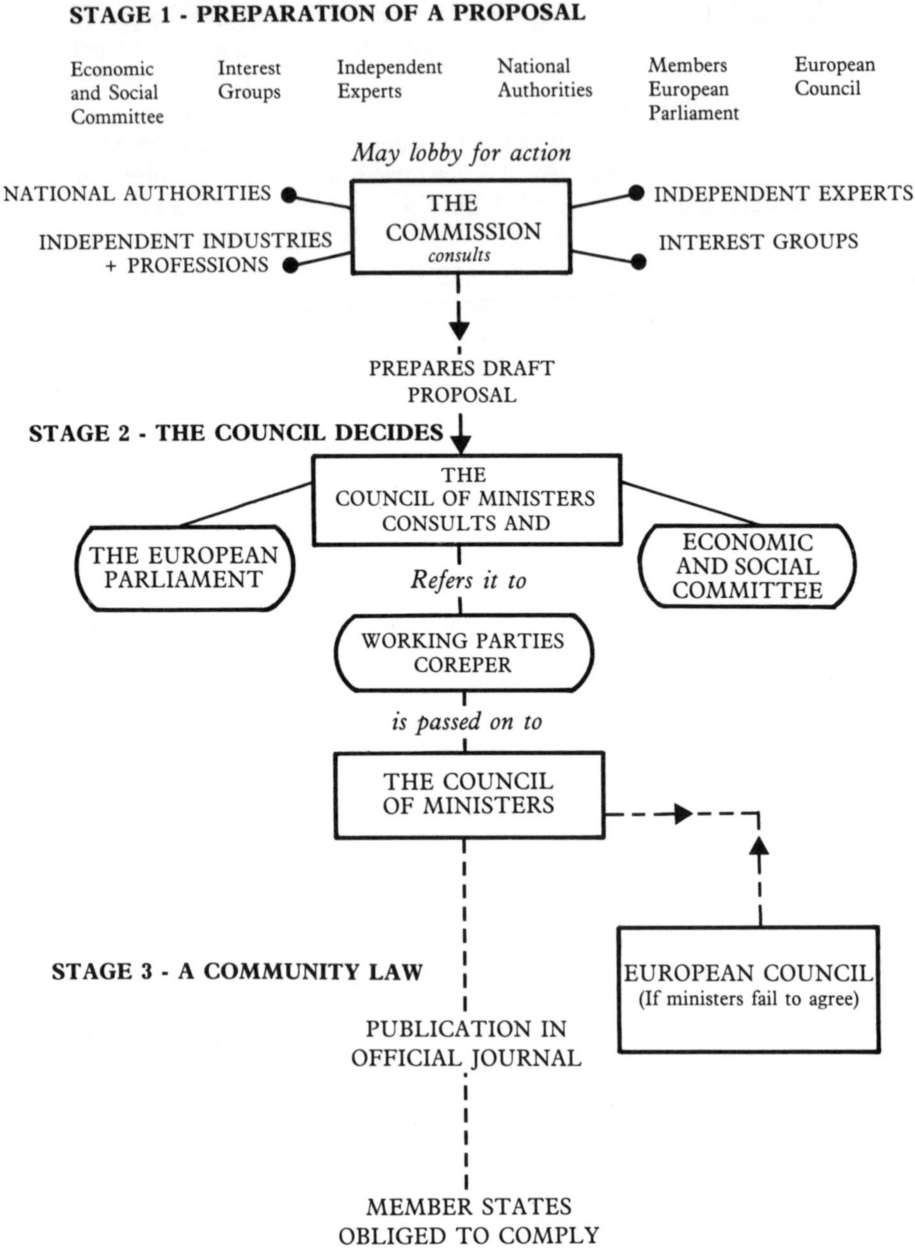

STAGE 1 - PREPARATION OF A PROPOSAL

Economic and Social Committee	Interest Groups	Independent Experts	National Authorities	Members European Parliament	European Council

May lobby for action

NATIONAL AUTHORITIES ●

INDEPENDENT INDUSTRIES
+ PROFESSIONS ●

THE
COMMISSION
consults

● INDEPENDENT EXPERTS

INTEREST GROUPS

↓

PREPARES DRAFT
PROPOSAL

STAGE 2 - THE COUNCIL DECIDES ↓

THE
COUNCIL OF MINISTERS
CONSULTS AND

THE EUROPEAN
PARLIAMENT

ECONOMIC
AND SOCIAL
COMMITTEE

Refers it to

WORKING PARTIES
COREPER

is passed on to

THE COUNCIL
OF MINISTERS

- - ▸

STAGE 3 - A COMMUNITY LAW

EUROPEAN COUNCIL
(If ministers fail to agree)

PUBLICATION IN
OFFICIAL JOURNAL

MEMBER STATES
OBLIGED TO COMPLY

to the discussion, but agreement is seldom reached on all points. A text is finally laid before COREPER which tries to settle outstanding differences. As they have considerable discretion, the permanent representatives often reach agreement where a working party fails. If COREPER agrees, the proposal goes before the Council of Ministers as an 'A' point on the agenda, to be agreed to without debate. If there are differences that COREPER has not been able to settle, the proposal is either sent back to the working party for further examination or forwarded to the Council for discussion by the ministers as a 'B' point. Whether it goes 'backwards' or 'forwards' depends on whether the difference is a technical one or a matter of policy. Divergences on policy can be reconciled only by the ministers.

THE COUNCIL DECIDES

The task of the Council is to take decisions on behalf of the Community and it is the responsibility of the ministers to resolve national differences on Commission proposals. If the Council wishes to amend the proposal, the amendment must have the unanimous consent of all ten members. The responsible commissioner attends the meeting to help the search for agreement. If agreement is reached, the proposal is put on the agenda of the next meeting of the ministers when it is formally adopted without debate. In order to comply with the Treaty requirements, the ministers will formally record a qualified majority vote in favour of the proposal. Once adopted, the proposal becomes a directive in Community legislation.

THE FINAL ARBITER

If the ministers fail to agree over a long period, the issue may be referred to one of the triennial meetings of the heads of government - the European Council - for resolution. If the European Council reaches agreement, it instructs the Council of Ministers to adopt the Commission's proposal according to the formal procedures laid down in the Treaty and described above.

A COMMUNITY LAW

The next stage of the legislative process is the publication of the directive in the *Official Journal of the European Communities*, from which date it becomes law. It is then up to each member state to implement whatever measures are needed at national level to give effect to the directive within the time limit laid down. If for any reason a member state fails to observe its obligations under the directive or misinterprets those obligations, the Commission may bring the offending country before the Court of Justice.

9
The Budget

MOST FAMILY SQUABBLES are over money. The EEC partners are currently engaged in a bitter dispute over how much each should pay and the return each should receive for its budget contribution. The member states, like most families, may resolve their differences amicably; if they do not, the result may be a broken Community.

OWN RESOURCES

Initially the Community was financed by contributions from the member states, although Article 201 of the Treaty of Rome allowed for more independent Community-based ways of financing its activities. The 1969 Hague summit decided to replace national contributions with a system of financing from the Community's own resources. The 'own resources' system consists of proceeds from customs duties, agricultural levies and up to 1% of the receipts of value added tax (VAT) collected in each member state. The new funding arrangement was set out in the

Luxembourg Treaty of 1970 but was not fully operational until 1978. Table 3 gives the share of each source of revenue in the Community budget for 1983. VAT receipts account for more than half of the Community's revenue.

Table 3
Percentage Share of Sources of Community Revenue, 1983

	%
VAT	55.4
Customs Duties	28.2
Agricultural Levies	9.3
Other (surplus from previous years, etc.)	7.1
	100.0

Source: Seventeenth General Report on the Activities of the European Communities.

Prior to 1970 when the Community was financed by annual grants from member states, the Parliament had no control over the level of Community expenditure. It could propose amendments to the draft budget each year but Council could reject these amendments by a qualified majority vote. The notion of democratic control over Community expenditure was maintained by the fact that the money each member state contributed had to be approved by the national parliament.

A direct effect of the new system agreed in 1970 was that national parliaments lost all control over Community financing. There was a strong argument for increasing the European Parliament's control by way of compensation for the loss of democratic control at national level. However, the Council of Ministers was reluctant to give the Parliament a real say in deciding the budget and the change introduced in 1970 in the procedure for agreeing the budget was a modest one. It was not until 1975 that Parliament was given a significant role in deciding the budget.

Under the new arrangements the Council drew a sharp distinction between expenses arising necessarily from the Treaty (obligatory expenditure) and other types of expenditure (non-obligatory expenditure). The distinction between the two is not always clear in practice and has been the source of argument between Council and Parliament. The division of the budget into obligatory and non-obligatory expenditure is determined

Diagram 2 - THE BUDGET CYCLE

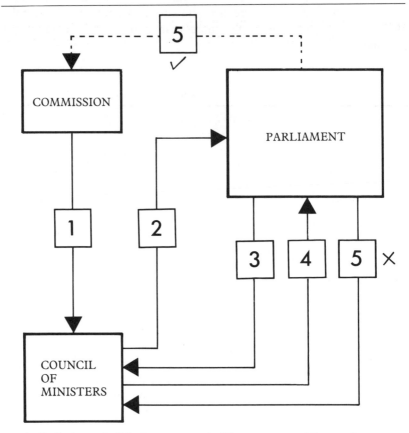

1 Preliminary draft budget
2 Draft budget
3 Proposed changes
4 Changes to non-obligatory items
5 Parliament either adopts (✓) or rejects (✗) budget

each year on a pragmatic basis by agreement between Parliament and the Council of Ministers. The first category of expenditure - obligatory - usually includes all funds required by the common agricultural policy, which is by far the greatest item of expenditure accounting for over 70% of all Community expenses. The remaining expenditure - non-obligatory - comprises spending under headings such as the social fund, staff administration and information costs of the Community.

BUDGET CYCLE

The 'budgetary authority' consists of Parliament and the Council. The preparation and adoption of the budget is governed by intricate details specified in the Treaty (see Diagram 2). At the beginning of each financial year the Commission draws up the major items of expenditure for inclusion in the following year's estimates. It then draws up provisional estimates, to which are added the estimates drawn up by the other institutions, and this first draft of the budget is sent to the Council by 15 June. After a maximum of forty-five days, the Council is required to refer the document to Parliament and it then becomes the draft budget. Parliament has forty-five days in which to consider it and to propose modifications in obligatory expenditure and amendments in the non-obligatory expenditure.

The draft budget goes back, together with these modifications and amendments, for consideration by the Council. The Council settles the items of obligatory expenditure. If the modifications increase the expenditure of the institution concerned the Council can simply refuse to accept them; if the proposed modifications do not increase the overall expenditure of the institutions the Council can reject the modification only by a qualified majority vote. Parliament has the power to adopt amendments to non-obligatory expenditure; it even has the power to increase expenditure under that heading, provided it stays within an overall financial limit agreed with the Commission.

When the Council has completed its work, the draft returns to the Parliament for final consideration. In 1975 it was made clear formally, in an amendment to the Treaties, that Parliament not only has the power to adopt the budget but also to reject the whole draft budget and to instruct the Council to submit a new draft. To reject the budget more than 50% of members of Parliament must vote, with a majority of two-thirds in favour of rejection.

Because of the many interests involved in the preparation of the budget there is close collaboration between Parliament and the Council. In 1975 a joint conciliation committee was set up representing Parliament, the Council of Ministers and the Commission. The committee attempts to reach a compromise or at least narrow the differences between the institutions as far as possible, within a maximum time of three months.

The Parliament is determined to be taken seriously in deciding Community priorities. It has criticised the budget for being little more than an accounting exercise for the common agricultural policy rather than a means of developing other policies necessary for economic integration.

Although the Commission tries to budget at the start of the year for expenditure over the following twelve months, it always has to look for more money through what is known as the supplementary budget. This is partly because the Commission has no control over decisions taken by the Council of Agriculture Ministers. If the ministers decide to raise the price of agricultural products, money has to be found even though the

Diagram 3 - SHARE OF COMMUNITY BUDGET - 1983

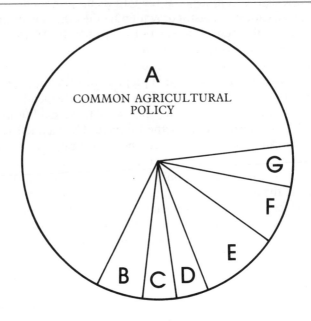

A Common Agricultural Policy	66%		**E** Regional Policy	9.5%
B Energy, Research, Industry, Transport	5.5%		**F** Social Policy	6.9%
			G Administration	5.0%
C Development Cooperation	4.3%			
D Refunds to Member States	4.1%			

Commission may disagree with the price rise. Diagram 3 shows how the Community's 1983 budget was broken down by sector and highlights the dominance of agricultural spending.

EUROPEAN CURRENCY UNITS

Because the member states have different currencies, subject to fluctuations vis-à-vis each other as well as outside currencies, the Community needs a standard unit for the purpose of accounting.

Following the establishment of the European monetary system in 1979 the unit of account used in Community financial transactions is known as the European currency unit (ECU). The value of the ECU is the sum of the values of a basket of currencies in which the relative weight of each is fixed. It is recalculated every day on the basis of market rates and published in the *Official Journal of the European Communities*. In February 1984 the ECU was worth seventy-two Irish pence.

THE FUNDS

The main financial instruments through which the Community spends money are the European agricultural guidance and guarantee fund (FEOGA), the social fund, the regional fund, the European development fund and the European Investment Bank. The Commission administers all the above funds with the exception of the Investment Bank. The reason for using a 'fund' in allocating grants is to allow money to be committed a number of years in advance. The Community adopted this practice from member states - in particular France, Germany and the Netherlands - which use funds for a variety of economic and social purposes. The use of funds grew out of criticism of the annual budgetary cycle of government which caused uncertainty and disruption in programmes which took longer than a year to complete.

Money is committed to the Community funds by the Council a number of years in advance. Every year the Community budget automatically includes a provision for each fund on the basis of the Council's multi-annual decision. This means that Parliament has little real say in the size of each of the funds. During 1978 Parliament challenged the fund system when it succeeded in increasing the allocation to the regional fund in the 1979 draft budget above the sum already agreed by the European Council and the Council of Ministers.

The total Community budget in 1983 was IR£18,044 million, of which Ireland's share was IR£184.7 million, or less than 1%. If Ireland's contribution seems large, it has to be set against the benefits which Ireland receives from the Community. In 1983 grants and subsidies to Ireland from the Community amounted to IR£707 million, or nearly four times the country's budget contribution. In addition, the Community approved loans for Ireland worth IR£282 million in 1982. Excluding loans, Ireland has received from the EEC nearly seven times the amount of her contributions to the budget from 1973 to 1982. As Table 4 shows, more than half of the transfers from the Community to Ireland were from the guarantee section of the common agricultural fund.

Table 4

Grants and Subsidies Approved for Ireland from European Community Funds

	1973 IR£M	1974 IR£M	1975 IR£M	1976 IR£M	1977 IR£M	1978 IR£M	1979 IR£M	1980 IR£M	1981 IR£M	1982 IR£M	1983 IR£M
FEOGA (guarantee section)	36.7	63.8	102.2	102.07	244.46	366.07	397.9	377.4	305.0	344.3	436.7
FEOGA (guidance section)	2.9	5.1	7.0	14.2	16.55	27.5	28.0	40.7	54.8	60.9	75.7
European social fund	4.1	7.0	9.4	13.0	19.70	29.8	38.5	53.5	73.0	97.0	91.9
European regional development fund	—	—	8.3	14.4	12.63	23.57	41.4	52.6	67.7	79.0	58.2
Other (incl. EMS interest subsidies)	0.1	0.4	0.6	1.3	1.24	0.123	44.38	48.0	50.68	53.3	44.6
Total grants and subsidies	43.8	76.3	127.5	144.97	294.58	447.063	550.18	572.2	551.18	634.5	707.1*
Contributions to the European Communities											
Total	6.1	7.5	10.4	16.5	21.8	42.0	60.36	91.56	112.215	136.7	184.7
Loans granted from Community sources to Ireland											
European Investment Bank (EIB)	11.1	24.8	22.0	35.4	52.1	78.5	226.1 *	252.8 *	237.0 *	281.7 *	218.2*
European Coal and Steel Community (ECSC)	0.21	—	1.21	—	0.17	0.123	17.5	3.1	7.8	0.03	—
Total	11.31	24.8	23.21	35.4	52.27	78.623	243.6	255.9	244.8	281.73	218.2

* Including New Community Instrument (NIC)

The responsibility for ensuring that Community monies are spent on the items for which they were allocated by the Council of Ministers and Parliament is the responsibility of the Court of Auditors.

The Court began operation in 1977 and consists of ten members, one from each member state. Its first president was Irish former senior civil servant, Michael N. Murphy, now an ordinary member. The Court has responsibilities at two levels. Firstly, it has to ensure proper financial control over Community spending - to this end it submits an annual report which is published in the *Official Journal of the European Communities*. The Court may at any time take the initiative of submitting observations on particular financial matters. It gained considerable publicity for its report on the excessive expense accounts of some commissioners. Secondly, it acts as a specialist advisory body to the Parliament in the exercise of its own function of control over the application of the budget. Since 1975, Parliament has had sole right to give final approval to the accounts of expenditure as submitted by the Commission.

The Court is empowered to carry out on-the-spot audits in the institutions of the Community and in the member states. At national level the audit is made in liaison with national audit offices or national departments. The Court may request any document or information necessary to its work from Community institutions, national governments or audit offices. One of the biggest problems faced by the Court is to decide whether money spent at national level was spent properly. If the Court feels that the money was improperly spent there are no procedures as yet for reclaiming the money from the member state.

BUDGET CRISIS

The Community entered 1984 with a major crisis over its ability to finance its policies. The money available under the 1% VAT ceiling was almost exhausted and there was no agreement on raising the VAT limit or on alternative sources of finance. Expenditure, particularly in the running of the common agricultural policy, threatened to exceed revenue. Since the Community has no power under the Treaty to fund its day-to-day operations by borrowing, the Commission proposed severe expenditure cuts in agriculture, including a super-levy on milk production in excess of 1981 output. Consequently, governments began difficult negotiations to work out a new financial settlement that would not only allow the Community to continue to operate present policies but also to develop fresh policies geared to the industrial and technological needs of the late twentieth century. Adding to the scale of the problem were the demands of Britain and West Germany for changes in the budget system that would reduce their net contributions. The need to take account of the cost to the Community of the accession of Spain and Portugal in the 1980s complicated the negotiations.

To resolve this crisis the Commission proposed an ambitious package of measures. It advocated abolishing the 1% VAT maximum and establishing a new ceiling of 2%. This could be approved only by amending the 1970 Treaty and by the ratification by national parliaments of the new settlement. Pending a better balance between agricultural and non-agricultural expenditure, the Commission proposed a 'modulation' of VAT revenues so that some countries would pay above - and others below - the Community VAT average. Three indicators would relate to agricultural output, national income per head and a member state's proportion of financial gains from Community membership.

At the European Council in Athens in December 1983, Mrs. Thatcher and Chancellor Kohl refused to approve the raising of the 1% VAT ceiling until farm surpluses were brought under control in a reform of agricultural expenditure - and until changes were made in the method of calculating national contributions to the Community budget. At their meeting in Brussels in April 1984 the heads of government were close to agreement on a settlement of the British rebate question, with only £75 million separating Britain from its partners. Since neither side was prepared to give way the meeting broke up in disarray and Britain afterwards withheld advance budget contributions to the Community.

Both London and Bonn argue that their 'net contribution' is too high. This means that their exchequer payments to Brussels exceed returns from the expenditure side of the Community budget. They feel aggrieved because, with the exception of France which averages out about even, the others do handsomely. Table 5 illustrates the gains and losses of member states from the Community budget.

Table 5

Gains and Losses of Member States from Community Budget, 1982

Measured in millions of European currency units: one equals IR£0.72.

	ECU (m)		ECU (m)
Belgium	+ 253	Ireland	+ 732
Denmark	+ 295	Italy	+1,616
West Germany	-2,085	Luxembourg	+ 256
Greece	+ 685	Netherlands	+ 304
		UK	-2,036

Since 1979 Mrs. Thatcher has complained that the budget system is unjust to Britain. After intensive campaigning she secured agreement on refunds of £645m for 1980, £783m 1981, £650m 1982 and £450m 1983 (proposed). Her complaint is directed against Belgium, Luxembourg, the Netherlands and Denmark who gained from the budget despite being richer than Britain. In effect, she is looking for 'a broad balance', that is that contributions should be more or less matched by expenditure returns. However, as British agriculture represents only 10% of all EEC production, it is difficult for the UK to obtain such returns as long as agriculture accounts for so much of the budget.

Ireland and France in particular contend that a fundamental principle of the Community is that 'own resources' belong to the Community and not to individual member states. They argue that to confine the discussion of Community financing to the budget is misleading. Membership of the Community has brought financial benefits to Britain which do not appear in the Community's accounts. In particular, Britain has access to the markets of the member states for her manufacturing products, a direct financial benefit of membership but one which does not appear in the annual budget.

In the short term, however, Britain wants a 'safety net' to prevent it being a net contributor as long as its per capita income is below a fixed level in relation to that of other member states. In the longer term, a solution for Britain and West Germany is for the budget to be restructured in a way that will enlarge spending on policies for the regions, and for employment, industry, transport and energy.

The Community row is not about such a vast amount of money as appears at first glance. Large by Irish standards, the Community budget is small in comparison to EEC gross domestic product or total public spending in member states - amounting to about 1% only. It was therefore with justification that Commission President Gaston Thorn could lament at the start of 1984: 'Are we prepared to sacrifice all that we have built and the prospects it offers for the future because of a budgetary quarrel, in which the money involved is chickenfeed beside the member states' own budgets? Absolutely not! I appeal to all Europeans of good faith.'

Mrs Thatcher is giving her EEC partners one last chance. If they do not come up with her £1 billion, or most of it by April, they will have to face the consequences. She is not threatening to leave the EEC; worse than that, she is threatening to stay in it.

The Irish Times editorial, December 1979

10
The Common Agricultural Policy

NO OTHER ASPECT of the Community has generated such controversy as the common agricultural policy (CAP). Its critics claim that it is costly, inefficient and bad economics. Its defenders agree that it is the worst agricultural policy - except for all the others. Both are right. The problem is to agree on a policy which will simultaneously guarantee plenty of food in the Community and an adequate income to farmers.

The attraction of the common agricultural policy was a major reason why Ireland joined the EEC. In the 1960s, before membership, Irish farmers sold four-fifths of their exports on the British market at prices well below those paid in the Community. British prices to the consumer were kept low by a policy of deficiency payments, or subsidies, paid to British farmers by their government. The large industrial population, the small size of the agricultural sector and the dependence of countries such as Ireland, Denmark and New Zealand on access to the British market meant that this policy worked well as far as Britain was concerned. However,

Britain was the only country in western Europe to pursue such a policy. In the common market agriculture was either an extremely important sector of the economy (Netherlands, France, Denmark, Italy) or the farming community was politically strong (West Germany). Membership of the Community offered a guaranteed market for an unlimited output of agricultural goods at much higher prices than Irish farmers had ever enjoyed before. The optimism on entry was justified, the period 1970-78 being the most prosperous in the history of Irish farming.

OBJECTIVES

Article 39 of the Treaty of Rome identified five objectives of a common agricultural policy: increased agricultural productivity, a fair standard of living for farmers, stabilised markets, assured supplies of food and maintenance of reasonable prices to the consumer. The CAP, agreed after difficult negotiations in 1962 when the Council of Ministers 'stopped the clock' to meet formal deadlines for decisions laid down in the Treaty, rests on three main principles - market unity, Community preference and financial solidarity.

MARKET UNITY

The aim of CAP is to ensure a single market in the member states for any commodity coming under its control by a system of common farm pricing throughout the Community. Prices for most of the main products originating in the Community are supported by 'target' and 'intervention' prices. The target price for a commodity is the price the member states agree should be aimed at in the Community. The intervention price, set at 5% to 20% below the target price, is what a producer is assured of receiving under the CAP for products. If the market price falls below the intervention price, the Community, through an intervention agency, supports the market and maintains price levels by offering producers the intervention price. Intervention prices are fixed for each product at the annual farm price review when the Council of Agriculture Ministers reconciles the claims of the farm lobby with the demands of some member states for reductions in CAP spending. Market unity and common pricing ensure that a tonne of butter or a gallon of milk are worth the same in every member state. This is an important principle but it has given rise to problems, discussed later.

COMMUNITY PREFERENCE

The CAP ensures that producers inside the Community are more favourably treated than producers outside the Community wishing to export to member states. Imports to the Community from third countries are controlled through 'threshold' prices which are related to the intervention price agreed for products produced within the Community. Exports to third countries receive export 'refunds' equivalent to the difference between the Community market price and the world price. This system of import levies and export refunds insulates the Community market from the world market and gives preference to Community producers.

FINANCIAL SOLIDARITY

The Treaty of Rome envisaged that the cost of organising agricultural markets would devolve on the Community, not on national governments. The January 1962 agreement established the European agricultural guidance and guarantee fund, usually known as FEOGA from its French initials. It is from this fund that the cost of supporting agricultural markets and restructuring farming is met.

CAP PRODUCTS

The first agricultural products to be regulated under the CAP were cereals, pigmeat, poultry and eggs. Only cereals enjoyed the full protection of target prices, intervention buying, import levies and export refunds. In December 1963 the Council agreed to regulate the market for dairy products, beet and rice in a similar way to cereals.

Dairy Products Dairy products have proved the most troublesome in the management of the CAP. By the mid-1970s half of FEOGA's expenditure on market support was going on dairy products, although it accounted for less than 20% of total agricultural production. Some member states are sensitive about this sector because it includes great numbers of small farmers with little alternative to milk production. The Irish government's concern about the dairy sector stems from its contribution to gross national product, over five times greater than the Community average. It is also the fastest growing sector in Irish agriculture, with milk output having increased by 50% between 1970 and 1981.

Beef When Ireland joined the EEC the demand for beef in the Community exceeded the supply. Because of the shortage and consequent high prices, the levy system on beef imports to the Community was greatly reduced while beef producers in member states were encouraged to expand production. After 1973 the oil-induced recession led to a decline in demand for expensive meat, particularly beef. The Council acted to safeguard Community producers in 1974 by imposing high levies on imports from third countries and by supporting exports from the Community. Irish beef exports to third countries have benefited greatly from Community support - Libya, Iraq and Iran becoming major buyers of Irish cattle. This trade has drawbacks - exporting live cattle reduces the job potential in the meat processing industry and the instability of the importing countries does not encourage confidence in the permanence of the markets. A feature of the market arrangements for beef is the controversial 'slaughter' premium which subsidises beef farmers in the UK and the 'suckler cow' premium which encourages producers to specialise in beef rather than dairy farming.

Other Products In 1968 new market structures were adopted for vegetable oils and oilseeds and after much controversy a system was agreed for sugar. Thus by July 1968, when the Community achieved full customs union, a single market had been created for practically all agricultural products with the main exceptions of wine, sheepmeat and potatoes. In 1970 agreement was reached on the organisation of wine and tobacco and eventually, in 1980, of sheepmeat. The CAP now covers about 90% of agricultural goods produced in the Community.

CHANGING THE STRUCTURE OF AGRICULTURE

The Community has attempted to improve the structure of agriculture in a half-hearted way but measures to date lack coherence. The most important directive covers the farm modernisation scheme (directive 72/169). Under this scheme participants are classified as 'commercial', 'development' and 'other'. Commercial farmers are those with incomes from farming equal to comparable earnings outside farming. Development farmers are those who can reach this level of income by implementing a development plan - the directive is primarily aimed at these farmers. Other farmers are those on holdings considered to be uneconomic. The scheme is primarily a system of subsidies towards capital investment, FEOGA support supplementing national funds. The Irish government has suspended the scheme temporarily to review its impact.

Directive 72/160 was introduced to encourage the transfer of land from older to development farmers. In 1975 an important directive (75/268) provided income aids to farmers in mountain, hill and other less favoured areas and many farmers in Connaught, Donegal, Cavan, Monaghan, Clare, Kerry and parts of other counties benefit from this. In 1978 there was a shift in Community policy towards helping designated areas which were suffering from chronic structural problems. The original aim was to help the Mediterranean area but the measures were extended to include Ireland and Northern Ireland. Of particular interest were the measures for land improvement and investment in the west of Ireland and a cross-border drainage scheme.

While these structural measures have brought important benefits to individual farmers they have done little to change the structure of agriculture in the Community or in Ireland. Agricultural expert Michael Tracy has commented that the key to structural adjustment is land mobility between farmers and this problem has not been solved. Nor has the problem of the relationship between structural change and market policy been solved, the objectives of structural schemes conflicting with the need to reduce surpluses. In 1977, for example, aid for buying cows under the farm modernisation plan was suspended to help reduce dairy surpluses and in 1980 the Council agreed in principle to restrict investment aids for dairy production.

The Community is also faced with new problems in this area. The assumption of continuing economic growth has been undermined. The absorption of surplus labour from farms by expanding industry can no longer be taken for granted. With growing unemployment in cities and towns the security of farm work provides at least some compensation for lower earnings. People have begun to question whether policies should encourage the transfer of rural population to already over-crowded and polluted cities. There has also been a reaction against intensive farming which has created many hazards in the environment. The result has been a sharp change in the Commission's approach. In 1983 it announced proposals to help small and uneconomic farmers to improve their farms; previously Community aid was directed at farmers who had the potential for attaining a relatively high level of income from farming. This change in approach may have great significance for farmers in the west of Ireland where much farming has been dismissed up to now as 'uneconomic'.

ADMINISTRATION

Overall responsibility for the management of the CAP rests with the Commission under powers delegated by the Council. A special administrative structure under the direction of the Commission was established to meet the special demands of managing the CAP. Because market conditions for agricultural goods can change from day to day, a flexible structure was needed to allow decisions to be taken quickly without reference to the Council. For each commodity under the CAP there is a management committee with a representative from each member state and chaired by the Commission. Only if the management committee fails to agree on what ought to be done will the issue be referred to the Council. This rarely happens. The Council remains responsible, however, for the most important decisions about the CAP. It is the agriculture ministers who decide the annual farm prices and agree new measures to reorganise the CAP.

Each member state plays an important role in the execution of the CAP through what are known as 'intervention agencies'. If the price for a commodity falls below a certain limit, the intervention agencies in the member states are obliged to buy the product, if offered for sale, at a special intervention price, store it until prices improve and subsidise exports to countries outside the EEC. In special cases the agency may subsidise sales within the EEC, as happens with butter. It is as a result of intervention buying that the so-called 'butter mountain' and 'wine lake' result. When production outstrips demand for a commodity, the Community finds it difficult to dispose of surpluses without undermining the income of producers. A substantial share of stocks bought in this way is sold within the Community when prices improve but the Community has accumulated a permanent surplus of dairy products, wine and beef. In recent times the Commission has made it more difficult to sell into intervention by delaying payments to suppliers. Since 1977 milk producers have had to pay a 'co-responsibility' levy in an effort to control the production of surplus milk and contribute to the cost of disposal. The levy is collected by the cooperatives to which the farmers sell their milk and this money is put towards the cost of administering the CAP.

Ireland, Luxembourg, Denmark and the UK have one intervention agency for all commodities. In Ireland and Luxembourg the Department of Agriculture is the intervention agency, while in the UK and Denmark the task has been assigned to a special intervention board. Other countries have more complicated arrangements. France has seven intervention agencies, the Netherlands eight. In some instances the agency may delegate its functions to other bodies. Expenditure incurred by the agency when intervening in markets and storing products is borne mainly by the Community. The chief cost falling on the national exchequer is the cost of administering the intervention agencies. In Ireland this means that the government pays the salaries and office expenses of those officials of the Department of Agriculture administering the CAP in Ireland. The Commission ensures that the individual agencies in the member states act in a coordinated way mainly through the mechanism of the management committees. The finance to operate the CAP is supplied through FEOGA. Expenditure is under two headings - guarantee payments and guidance payments. The guarantee section covers the cost of support and intervention policies and accounts for by far the largest share of expenditure from FEOGA . Most money is spent on milk, milk products and cereals and, to a lesser extent, on sugar, beef, veal, olive oil and oilseeds. The guidance section of FEOGA provides part of the money for structural policies designed to increase efficiency and improve the rural infrastructure. One feature of structural spending is that it is incurred over a period of years, reflecting the long-term nature of many of the schemes.

THE GREEN POUND

The application of common agricultural prices in the original six member states required a common accounting unit. The 'unit of account' was devised as the common denominator between the currencies of the six, now ten, member states. Common prices are fixed in units of account while the actual transactions, such as intervention buying and payments to producers, are carried out in national currencies. Units of account are translated into a national currency by applying a fixed exchange rate to the price expressed in units of account. The exchange rate applied to the Irish transaction is known, rather misleadingly, as the 'green pound'. In the early years of the CAP the member states' currencies were stable. The currencies of the Six and the unit of account were valued against gold and it was a simple operation to translate national currencies into units of account. The value of each currency for transactions under the CAP was the same as on the currency markets.

MONETARY COMPENSATORY AMOUNTS

The monetary instability of the late 1960s caused problems for the CAP. Monetary compensatory amounts (MCAs) were introduced to protect the principle of market unity in the face of fluctuating currencies and the absence of a common Community currency. It is fundamental to the success of the CAP that the price agreed for a product at the annual farm price review should apply in all member states for the following year. When, after 1969, member states' currencies began to revalue and devalue against each other this principle was threatened. In 1969 France devalued the franc by 11%. A French farmer or trader could increase income dramatically by bringing produce across the border to Germany, selling it for German marks and buying more francs with the stronger marks. It was a choice between closing the border to agricultural produce or introducing a mechanism which would limit windfall benefits to traders from currency fluctuations. The Commission's solution was to introduce MCAs, which were levies imposed at the French border on agricultural goods moving to other member states. The levies neutralised the potential to the French trader of the devaluation of the franc. The system was extended later to cover the problem caused by the revaluation of the German mark. MCAs in this case acted as a subsidy on agricultural goods from Germany to other member states to ensure their competitiveness.

The MCA resulting from a currency devaluation is known as a 'negative' MCA to distinguish it from the 'positive' MCA arising from a currency re-valuation. A temporary expedient, MCAs soon became a permanent feature of the CAP. MCAs should have been phased out at the annual farm price reviews by devaluing or revaluing the 'green' rates of exchange, but a reduction in 'positive' MCAs means a fall in support prices in the member state concerned, making realignment politically difficult. Towards the end of the 1970s, the gap between the market and green rates of exchange for some currencies was very marked. In October 1976 the difference between the market and green rates for sterling was 37%. The UK refused to devalue the green rate because this would have meant an increase in food prices to the consumer which was unacceptable to the British Labour government. Because of the divergence between British and Irish policy on this issue, it was agreed in 1976 that Ireland would have its own green rate of exchange. When sterling was losing its value against other currencies, it suited Irish farmers to have the green rate as close as possible to the market rate in order to sell competitively within Europe. The scope for devaluing the green rate was greatly reduced by the decision to join the European monetary system. By 1980 the stability of exchange rates within the EMS lessened the possibility of further increases in income for farmers through adjustments of the green rate.

The Commission has put pressure on member states to phase out MCAs because of the long-term distortions in agriculture which result from their use. One effect of MCAs is to subsidise farming in countries with a revalued currency. German farmers can buy oil and fertiliser cheaper because the mark is worth more on the world market. Then they receive a subsidy in the form of an MCA which allows them to compete against farmers in countries with a weak currency. Farmers in Ireland, on the other hand, have to pay more for farm inputs because the Irish pound is worth less on world markets but they are prevented from taking advantage of a weak currency when selling goods by having to pay a levy on goods exported to countries such as Germany. The natural advantages of climate and soil that Irish farmers enjoy in producing milk and beef are reduced by the MCA system. Without MCAs many dairy farmers in Germany would not be able to stay in business and would be forced to change from dairy farming or to leave agriculture.

IMPACT OF THE CAP ON IRELAND

The main effect of the CAP on Irish agriculture so far has been a monetary one. This is clearly seen by a comparison between farm income in the 1960s and 1970s. In the 1960s farm income was stagnant and farmers fell further behind other income groups. The ratio of average farm income per head to industrial wages fell by just over 7%. In the period 1970-78 on the other hand, aggregate farm income increased by 72%, after allowing for inflation. As people continued to leave agriculture, this meant that average farm income more than doubled during these eight years. Farmers experienced a big gain in income relative to wage earners, while continuing to bear a relatively lighter share of taxation. Since 1979, however, farm income has fallen sharply due to a combination of lower price increases, high interest rates and inflation.

The increase in farming income in the 1970s was due mainly to higher prices for farm products. Prices for Irish agricultural products increased 4½ times between 1970 and 1978. It is easy to see why successive governments have favoured higher prices under the CAP. For every IR£100 gained by a farmer from a price increase, IR£70 is paid by consumers in other member states and only IR£30 by Irish consumers. The increased export earnings justify higher prices to Irish consumers - and the decision to remove VAT from food in 1973 was intended to cushion the blow of higher prices to the Irish consumer. The money earned from agricultural products in the Community was a major contributor to the 23% increase in the volume of the country's gross national product between 1972 and 1978.

Apart from stimulating milk production, the unprecedented increase in farm prices seems to have had little impact on the structure of Irish agriculture. One immediate but short-term effect was an increase of 233% in the average price per acre of agricultural land between 1970 and 1979. But there has been no acceleration in the growth rate of agriculture and there has been little change in the use of resources. People are not leaving the land in any greater numbers than they did in the 1960s. Despite deep-seated problems in the organisation of farming in many areas, the Community's structural policies have had little impact. Directive 72/160 on the retirement of elderly farmers, for example, never got off the ground, partly because the pension paid to farmers under the scheme is IR£1,344 per year while they can gain IR£450 more by claiming the non-contributory old age pension and remain in possession of the farm.

Until recently the dairy sector was successful in finding markets in other member states and outside the Community, but faced in 1982 with surpluses which they could not sell, dairy farmers sold much produce into intervention. The beef sector is probably more disorganised now than before entry. Ireland produces six times more beef than it can consume and needs an aggressive export policy if the meat is to be sold abroad. Beef producers have been unable to overcome the problems of over-supply in a declining market. Intervention buying has become a permanent feature of the regime in Ireland.

BRITAIN AND THE CAP

As the Community's most developed policy, the CAP accounts for the largest share of Community spending, amounting to 65% of the budget in 1983. The effect of spending under the CAP is to transfer money from countries with large industrial populations and small farming sectors - Britain and West Germany - to member states with substantial farm sectors - Ireland, the Netherlands and Denmark. Since 1979 the British government has argued that its contribution to the Community is imbalanced because the financial benefits it receives from the CAP are small by comparison with the bill it has to pay for food.

Member states have argued in reply that Britain's payments under the CAP are a small price to pay in return for access to the industrial markets of the Ten and are cheaper than the old system of deficiency payments by which the UK used to organise its food policy. If the British argument were accepted, it would undermine one of the cornerstones of the CAP - the notion of financial solidarity among member states in meeting the costs of the policy.

A compromise was reached in 1980 which concedes the British point on the question of financial imbalance without conceding the principle of financial solidarity under the CAP. It was agreed that Britain would be given rebates on her budget contributions, to be agreed annually and to be spent on projects approved by the Community to which the British would also have to contribute part of the cost. While this provides a temporary settlement, the British want a permanent solution which would reduce spending on the CAP.

REFORMING THE CAP

There is general agreement that the CAP has been successful in securing food supplies and in maintaining incomes for the EEC's eight million farmers. However, the pricing policy of the CAP has encouraged permanent surpluses of products, particularly in the dairy sector. There is growing opposition to paying for agricultural goods which nobody wants to eat or drink.

Prolonged recession has dampened consumer spending power and demand for expensive foodstuffs. The population trend in the Community compounds these economic changes. The rate of population growth in member states slowed to a negligible 0.2% in the latter half of the 1970s. In recent years consumption of agricultural goods has increased by only 0.5% per year. At the same time agriculture has become more efficient. While the end of the recession may increase demand for farm products, slow population growth will limit the scope for increasing consumption within the Community. Nor is there much prospect of increasing food exports to the rest of the world. As a result the Community is threatened with a surplus of twenty million tonnes of milk, costing the EEC budget about IR£4 billion to support. Agriculture expert, Professor Seamus Sheehy, has calculated that to maintain real prices for CAP products at their 1982 level, the EEC budget would have to increase almost three-fold in real terms by 1990. Since this is out of the question, the Community is faced with the problem of reforming the CAP.

In Stuttgart on 18 June 1983 the heads of government decided on reform. In July 1983 the Commission presented the Council with far-reaching proposals, the main thrust of which was to end the Community's unlimited guarantee to farmers of price and intervention support for agricultural produce. The Commission proposed also that producers would have to accept greater responsibility for the cost of disposing of surpluses beyond an agreed threshold. The proposals were designed as a package, some of which were favourable to Ireland and others which aroused fundamental objections. Favourable to Ireland were the proposed controls on import of cereal substitutes, the removal of UK aids to beef producers, the reduction of imports from New Zealand, a tax on the consumption of oils and fats other than butter and the phased elimination of MCAs. But in Irish eyes the benefits of these measures were more than outweighed by the Commission's proposal to impose a supplementary levy on surplus production of milk above 1% of total deliveries in 1981. This 'super-levy', calculated to cover the cost of disposal, would be charged on milk deliveries in excess of a quota established for each milk plant. This policy would have meant a cut in production in Ireland of about 13.5% and a loss of more than IR£100 million to the economy.

Irish farmers vehemently opposed the super-levy and the quota on milk production on the grounds that Ireland had not yet reached its potential in dairy farming. The average milk yield per cow in the Community is 915 gallons a year while the Irish average - and rising fast - is 750 gallons. In addition, 1981 was a particularly poor year for Irish milk production because of unfavourable weather conditions.

The Government was equally opposed to the super-levy because of the importance of dairying, the country's chief export earner, to gross national product and the growth of the economy. Taoiseach Dr. FitzGerald argued that if the super-levy as proposed by the Commission were imposed, Ireland would bear a financial burden twenty times greater than that which the EEC regarded as an unfair imposition on Britain. The government informed its partners that it considered that a vital national interest was at stake and that it was prepared to use the veto to block the Commission's CAP reform package if necessary. The most critical and difficult negotiations for Ireland since accession had begun.

Prior to the European Council meeting in December 1983, Dr. FitzGerald met each of the heads of government to impress upon them the strength of Irish opposition to the super-levy. The EEC leaders were accompanied in Athens by their foreign and agriculture ministers in an attempt to resolve simultaneously the complex and interrelated problems facing the Community. The European Council, however, broke up in disarray over Britain's budgetary contribution. In January 1984 the French assumed the presidency of the EEC and made the resolution of the crisis in the Community a priority. Before the next meeting of the European Council on 19 March, President Mitterrand toured the capitals of the member states in a search for compromise. This led to a breakthrough at the Council of Agriculture Ministers when, days before the premiers were due to meet, the Commission's package was agreed in principle. Austin Deasy, Irish Minister for Agriculture, emphasised that his government's agreement was conditional on acceptance that the Irish case for a quota-free expansion of the dairy industry would be decided by the heads of government. Any hopes that the Irish government may have had of a quick recognition of their case were dashed at the European Council meeting in Brussels when a compromise proposal, acceptable to the Irish government and put forward by the French president, was curtly dismissed by the British and Dutch premiers. Emphasising the depth of Irish feeling on the issue, Dr. FitzGerald took the unprecedented step in the European Council of gathering up his papers and walking out of the meeting.

This controversial gesture seems to have had the intended effect of concentrating the minds of the Council on meeting Irish difficulties. On Saturday 24 March, Mr. Dalsager, Commissioner for Agriculture, and Michel Rocard, French Minister for Agriculture and President of the Agriculture Council, arrived in Dublin to seek a compromise solution. But it seemed that there was no way of reconciling the Irish objective of permitting milk production to increase at the rate achieved per annum - 5% per annum - with the other members' demand that the unpalatable medicine of the super-levy be swallowed equally by all member states. The member states which had agreed to cut their milk production by between 3% and 8% under the Commission's proposals had incurred intense domestic opposition which could only worsen if concessions were made to Ireland.

When the agriculture ministers met to decide the farm package on 26 March, Mr. Deasy met such resistance to the Irish demands that he was forced to invoke the Luxembourg compromise on vital national interests and veto agreement on the Commission's proposals. The government's determination to maintain the veto was put to the test in the following week as pressure built up on the government to accept minimal concessions offered by the other member states. The Irish case was weakened by the prospect that if there were no agreement on CAP reform, the related budget issue could not be solved. The Community would be unable to meet its commitments under the CAP and farmers would be faced with severe cuts in income. Under such circumstances, pressure would mount on member-state governments to reintroduce national aids to farmers and the principles of a unified market and financial solidarity would be undermined. Irish farmers would be the chief losers if the CAP were weakened. Furthermore, the government cannot have relished the thought that if the French presidency, with its power and influence, failed to solve the crisis in the Community, the baton would pass to the Irish presidency in July 1984. The prospect of presiding over the possible collapse of the CAP was a daunting one for any Irish government to contemplate. For the first time in many years there was talk of out-voting Ireland on the issue of the super-levy at the Council of Ministers, despite the recognition of a vital national interest.

The Irish nerve held however, and, in the early hours of Saturday 30 March, the other member states conceded the substantial part of the Irish demands. It was agreed that Irish milk production would be allowed to increase in 1984 by 4.6% on 1983 levels before any levy would be imposed. Since production in the other member states was not allowed to rise much above 1981 levels, this was a major concession by the nine partners. Equally significant was a promise of an annual review of the level of milk production, agreement that Ireland would have priority in the Community if additional production were allowed and a guarantee that Irish milk production would not be reduced below the level agreed for this year. While Joe Rea, the President of the Irish Farmers' Association, denounced the agreement as 'totally inadequate', the package seems a reasonable compromise between the interests of Ireland and those of the Community and is much better than many feared the government would be forced to accept. It also led to agreement on the other proposals of the Commission's reform package, particularly the reduction or 'clawback' on the subsidies paid to British farmers on beef exports, which will restore the competitiveness of Irish beef exports against UK competitors. The agreement also involved the dismantling of MCAs and small increases in farm prices. The threat to the future of the CAP was removed and the way opened for agreement on Britain's budgetary contributions and for increasing the Community's 'own resources'.

Only one-third of Irish dairy farmers are actually expanding their output of milk; the remainder are either declining or have reached a stable level. Following the March agreement it is up to Irish farmers to ensure that milk production expands by 4.56% on the 1983 level to ensure a strong bargaining position in the 1985 review of milk production in the Community. In the longer term it may be more profitable for Irish farmers to concentrate on the quality of their dairy products rather than on quantity if they are to maintain and expand their market share.

11
Fisheries

BLUE EUROPE

THE ADOPTION BY the Community of a revised twenty-year common fisheries policy on 25 January 1983 brought to a successful conclusion difficult and long negotiations which more than any other aspect of EEC membership aroused public controversy and opposition in Ireland, not least from the Irish Fishermen's Organisation. A principal creator of this 'Blue Europe' policy was Donegalman Eamonn Gallagher, Director General of Fisheries of the Commission, and the agreement was signed for Ireland by the Minister for Fisheries, Paddy O'Toole. The agreement provides a framework for the development of the Irish fishing industry.

It was no coincidence that the Six began to think about a fisheries policy when Ireland, Britain, Denmark and Norway - countries with extensive fish stocks - applied to join the Community. The Six agreed that a basic principle underlying the policy would be equal conditions of access to fish stocks for the fleets of member states in each other's territorial waters - there was to be a 'Community pond'. Largely based on the model of the common agricultural policy, the fisheries policy made provision for marketing and price support as well as making grants available for the construction and modernisation of boats.

Next to Japan and the Soviet Union, the EEC fishing fleet has the largest fish catch in the world. Although the fishing sector is relatively small in job numbers, most of the Community's 160,000 fishermen are from the peripheral regions of the Community. Fishing is most important to Ireland and Denmark and least important to Belgium and West Germany as a proportion of gross domestic product. With under 2% of the total EEC catch in 1973 and the smallest fleet, Ireland's fishing industry was underdeveloped. This was the case despite growth in the decade before joining the EEC when the number of fishermen rose by about 50%, the landings tripled, the fleet grew and investment in fish processing increased. In 1965 the fleet consisted of 1,812 vessels of which thirty-six were over sixty feet; by 1974 it had grown to 2,420, of which 153 were over sixty feet. Fishing was mainly inshore. Killybegs, the largest port, is in Donegal, one of the poorest areas of the Community.

While the trade prospects for Irish fisheries in an enlarged Community were attractive the equal access principle became a point of contention. There was particular anger in the applicant countries that the big trawlers of the Six, which had overfished their own waters, would be able 'to fish up to the beaches'. A compromise was reached during accession negotiations, however, giving Ireland and Britain a ten-year exemption from the free access rule. Only countries which had traditionally fished in the six-mile zone around the coastline, were to be allowed to continue fishing there. The six-mile limit was extended to twelve miles from Lough Foyle to Cork Harbour on the west coast, and from Carlingford Lough to Carnsore Point on the east for shellfish. Britain obtained a twelve-mile limit off the coastal waters of county Down. Before the end of the ten-year period the Commission was to review 'the economic and social development of the coastal areas of the member states and the state of stocks' and the Council was to agree new arrangements. This review clause was not enough to prevent Norway voting against entry in a referendum.

Seven years before that review was due, however, the fisheries policy once again became a major controversy among the member states. In October 1975 Iceland declared a 200-mile protected zone around its coast to the detriment in particular of the British long-distance fleet. During 1976 it became clear that the United States, the Soviet Union, Canada and Norway would follow the Icelandic example. Thus in November 1976 the member states of the Community agreed to extend to 200 miles their fisheries zones in the North Sea and the North Atlantic from January 1977.

At the same time the Commission became alarmed at the scientific evidence showing that a large number of fish stocks in the Community's 200-mile zone had become critical. Overfishing in the previous twenty years had endangered many species including herring. Losses of fishing rights in the extended territorial waters of non-EEC states was also a blow to the Community, 30% of whose total catch (about 1.4 million tonnes) was in third-country waters. Because the bulk of the enlarged Community waters in the North Sea and the Atlantic were under Irish and British jurisdiction, the governments in Dublin and London began to demand fifty-mile exclusive zones to satisfy the vocal fish lobbies, but the Commission insisted that such demands were unrealistic.

In The Hague, in October 1976, Minister for Foreign Affairs Garret FitzGerald won a recognition of the Irish fishing industry's right to expand, specifically by doubling the catch between 1977 and 1979. Dr. FitzGerald announced that the government's development plan aimed to double landings of sea fish by 1979, bringing the total to 150,000 tonnes. To achieve this the fleet would be increased by some 300 vessels. Processing and other shore-based services would be expanded and the number employed by the industry was forecast to rise by 2,500 from the 1976 figure of 9,300 to 11,800. It was the government's objective to raise the numbers to 18,000 in the near future.

Despite the Community's acceptance of Ireland's special case, the coalition government in February 1977 introduced a national conservation measure prohibiting boats of over thirty-three metres in length or 1100 brake horse power from fishing in inshore Irish waters. After angry diplomatic exchanges between member states, the Commission took Ireland to the Court of Justice, which ruled that the measure was discriminatory as it excluded fishermen from other states. Ireland withdrew the measure, despite renewed calls by fishermen for an exclusive fifty-mile zone.

To soften the territorial demands of the Irish and British governments, the Commission drew up proposals in May 1977 to run the policy on a system of fishing plans. This did not satisfy British Fisheries Minister John Silkin who demanded a twelve-mile exclusive zone and a 'dominant preference' in the twelve to fifty-mile stretch. Mr. Silkin refused to attend an informal meeting of the fisheries ministers in West Berlin at the end of January 1978 at which Fianna Fáil's Brian Lenihan officially dropped Ireland's fifty-mile claim. Mr. Lenihan said he was satisfied that 'substantial advantage' would be secured through a scheme for fishing plans operating on an interim basis and designed to offer special preference for Irish fishermen up to 200 miles from the coast.

Despite progress in Berlin, negotiations on an overall common policy were not completed until early 1983. In the meantime fishing was regulated by nationally coordinated measures, on an annual basis. During that time too the shape of the policy took form with Ireland securing about IR£15 million in grants for the fishing industry under interim measures agreed annually between 1977 and 1982. The Community also agreed to provide IR£30 million for surveillance on sea and in the air. With the exception of herring (a ban was introduced in the Celtic Sea off the south-east coast to preserve stocks from extinction) the catch quotas for Ireland were increased along The Hague lines. Although Britain and France reached agreement on the question of access by early 1982, adoption of a comprehensive fish policy was held up by the Danes until January 1983. Under the new policy Ireland was allocated 4.3% of species subject to quota restrictions in all EEC waters. This amounted to 149,485 tonnes, of which 41,485t were white fish, 80,000t mackerel and 28,000t herring. When herring stocks recover, Ireland's quota will rise to 60,000t, or 15% of that stock total. Most Community fish are in the North Sea and other areas where Irish fishermen have not fished. Thus the 4.3% figure is not so small as it looks - it ensures a doubling of the 1975 catch. Agreement on 1984 quotas was reached in January 1984 providing, in Ireland's case, for 85,300 tonnes of mackerel, 27,170t of herring, 11,520t of cod, 3,060t of saithe, 555t of sole, 3,070t of plaice, 17,800t of whiting and 4,370t of haddock, 2,200t of monk and 2,000t of megrim.

THE MAIN GROUND-RULES OF THE POLICY

Access to Stocks Equality of access to resources was reaffirmed as the basic principle of the policy but preferential arrangements for inshore fishermen were set out for twenty years with the possibility of alterations being made at the end of ten years. This ensured an exclusive six miles around the coast for Irish fishermen with the range band extending to twelve miles off the Donegal and Kerry coasts. Fishing rights in certain areas between six and twelve miles off the coast where they had fished before were granted to French, British, Dutch, German and Belgian waters where they had traditional rights.

Conservation and Management Conserving and managing the stocks is governed by a system of total allowable catches (TACS), which is fixed annually by the Council of Ministers. Scientific evidence is taken into account about species threatened by overfishing when TACS are calculated. Available stocks are then distributed among the member states on a quota basis that includes such criteria as traditional fishing, the employment dependency of a region on fisheries and compensation for losses in the fishing grounds of non-member states. As part of the policy for conserving stocks, Community standards are applied to fishing gear - specifying minimum mesh sizes for nets, as well as setting catch limits and designating closed seasons for fisheries in certain areas. A logbook must be kept by skippers of fishing vessels flying the flag of a member state or registered in a member state. This logbook gives details of the fish caught and the tackle used. An inspection force was set up of Commission agents to oversee control operations carried out by the national authorities at sea and in ports.

Common Organisation of the Market Common standards for the marketing of fish and shellfish help producer organisations by fixing guide prices and withdrawal prices, the latter fluctuating between 70% and 90% of the guide price. A limited number of grants is available for improved fish processing so as to avoid resorting to intervention disposal of stocks. There is protection too from imports of fish from outside the Community, when these fall below the EEC reference price level.

Modernisation About IR£180 million was allocated for three years for grant-aiding of conversion and modernisation projects. These include grants for exploratory fishing and for the scrapping of boats no longer in use.

International Relations The Community's power to conclude fishery agreements with third countries and to sign international agreements on behalf of member states was confirmed. There are framework agreements with Norway, the Faroes and Sweden with which catch quotas are fixed annually on a reciprocal basis. An agreement with the United States enables EEC fleets to fish stocks which cannot be fished by American trawlers. A six-year agreement was signed with Canada. The Community has entered into agreements with developing countries such as Senegal, Guinea and Guinea-Bissau under which it obtains fishing rights in return for development grants.

In an address to the Irish Council of the European Movement in May 1983 Eamonn Gallagher described the common fisheries policy as the second integrated European policy and, in several respects, a more sophisticated one than the common agricultural policy. Firstly, unlike agriculture where member states retain certain competence, fisheries are an exclusive competence of the Community. For this reason the Community itself is the only representative of Community interests in international fisheries conventions. Secondly, through the system of TACS and quotas, the common fisheries policy has installed a limit on production of the main fish species and, through control regulation, requires the member states to ensure respect for these production limits. Thirdly, the medium-term structural policy is a larger feature, comparatively speaking, of the common fisheries policy than is the structural policy in the agricultural sector.

As it stands, however, the common fisheries policy is incomplete and is bound to evolve, especially when the 'armadas' of Spain and Portugal make the Community fleet the second largest in the world after the Soviet Union, roughly doubling the number of Community fishermen.

12
Industry

TOWARDS A UNIFIED MARKET

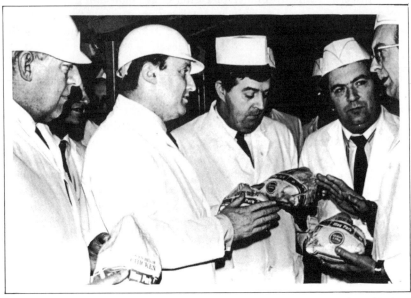

Commissioner Tugendhat discusses market prospects with Ian Paisley, John Taylor, John Hume and businessman Trevor Campbell.

THE SINGLE most important task of the EEC is to create a unified market for the manufacture and distribution of industrial goods. Other Community policies aim to promote this goal or to modify the consequences for disadvantaged groups or regions. It is surprising then that the Community has no common industrial or commercial policies but only an array of measures which it uses to steer industry and national governments towards the objectives of the Treaty.

The Six committed themselves to free trade in goods within a common customs union and external tariff and to the removal of all technical barriers to trade. The Commission was to enforce free competition among firms in the Community, outlaw cartels and monopolies which abused their power and prevent governments from unfairly helping domestic industry or agriculture. The governments also promised to remove the many restrictions on the movement of workers, services and capital within the EEC. Power to coordinate the fiscal, economic and industrial policies of the members and to establish complementary transport and commercial policies was given to the Community by the Treaty, but it was vague on the details of how this was to be done.

While the Six were shaping the common market, the Irish government was reassessing its economic and industrial policies. Since the 1930s Irish industry was protected behind high tariff barriers from foreign imports. Designed to foster native industry and employment in the depressed conditions of the 1930s the policy by the 1950s had outlived its usefulness. Irish manufacturing industry, primarily geared to the home market, could not expand sufficiently to provide full employment or the level of investment necessary for economic growth.

The movement from protection to free trade was accompanied by policies which aimed to help Irish industries export abroad and to attract foreign industry to Ireland. This trend was confirmed by government commitment to economic planning, principally by using the public capital programme to stimulate prosperity. The years 1959-61 have been described by Dr. T. K. Whitaker as the crunch period in Ireland's move to free trade, with Ireland seeking membership of the General Agreement on Tariffs and Trade and the European Community. Although disappointed by France's rejection of Britain's application, the government continued to work on the assumption that Ireland would one day be a member. In 1965 Anglo-Irish agreement provided for the progressive removal of Irish protection against UK imports and also gave farmers freer access to British markets. When Ireland joined the EEC in 1973 it was in the final stages of implementing the free-trade ageement with Britain. Ireland's entry coincided with a downward trend in the world economy. This cyclical dip was followed by the embargo of the oil-exporting countries which threw the industrial nations into the worst economic recession since the 1930s. It is against this background that Ireland's economic performance in Europe has to be assessed.

Official expectations about the effects of membership for Irish industry were high. The 1972 White Paper believed that it would encourage firms to diversify into new markets and attract into the country non-EEC based firms wanting to export to the vast Community market without having to pay the common external tariff. Employment in manufacturing industry was expected to rise by 50,000, any losses in existing firms being compensated for by job creation in new industries. This estimate was largely shared by business but was disputed by trade unionists who feared job losses in manufacturing of between 30,000 and 35,000. The alternatives to membership suggested during the referendum campaign involved some form of free trade, either in a special agreement with the Community or with the European Free Trade Association (EFTA). A return to the protectionism of the 1930s was not seen as a serious option.

Under the terms of accession, tariffs on Irish goods and goods from other member states entering the Community were phased out in five equal steps of 20% between 1 April 1973 and 1 July 1977. Quotas on imports were phased out by July 1975. Tariffs and quotas were also eliminated against countries with which the EEC had preferential trade arrangements. The Irish government was obliged to open tenders for public contracts to firms of all member states. The most important concession won by the government in negotiations concerned car assembly. The industry was permitted to retain a measure of protection against competition from other member states for twelve years, until the end of 1984.

Shortly after accession, Irish industry suffered an incalculable loss. On their way home from a meeting in Brussels twelve of the country's leading industrialists, including Con Smith, Michael Sweetman and Ned Grey, were killed when the plane in which they were travelling crashed at London airport. Their tragic deaths removed a generation of leaders of Irish industry in a country where entrepreneurial and industrial talent are in short supply.

Since accession, the performance of Irish industry in the Community has been well below the expectations of 1972. Output from manufacturing industry in the period 1972-82 was lower than levels achieved in the previous decade. Employment, far from rising as anticipated, was the same in 1982 as it was in 1972. This stability in the overall level of jobs conceals major differences between sectors. Particularly hard hit were indigenous Irish industries supplying clothes, textiles and footwear to the home market and using outdated technology and unskilled labour. These firms were unable to withstand the competition from more efficient British firms and, to a lesser extent, from Third World imports. It has been estimated that 40% of manufacturing jobs in industries such as these were lost between 1973 and 1983. The special arrangements for car assembly were insufficient to ensure the survival of the industry - all firms, including Fords, the largest and longest established, closing before the twelve-year deadline expired.

However, the performance of Irish industry in the decade 1972-82 was better than the EEC average. The poor performance of some Irish firms was more than compensated for by the strength of others, particularly export-oriented industries. The growth of these firms and the decline of native Irish firms has brought about a transformation of Irish industry, aided by accession to the Community. By 1980 foreign firms accounted for one-third of manufacturing industry and 70% of manufactured exports, in sharp contrast with the position thirty years previously. While British imports increased their share of the Irish market, fears that accession would bring a flood of imports from the other seven were not realised. Thanks mainly to agricultural exports, Ireland maintains a healthy balance of trade with its continental partners. According to Liam Connellan of the Confederation of Irish Industry, it is highly probable that, had Ireland been outside the Community during the recession of the last decade, manufacturing employment would be significantly lower than at present.

The Community has also brought tax advantages to firms manufacturing for the home market. Prior to 1980 firms exporting manufactured goods enjoyed the advantages of the export sales relief, which meant that they paid no tax on profits earned from exports. The Commission argued that this sales relief was unfair to industries selling only to the home market, and in 1980 the tax on profits of all manufacturing firms in Ireland was reduced to 10%. This tax, which is only one-fifth of what equivalent firms in other member states have to pay and is a major concession to Ireland by the Commission, applies to all firms producing for the home market and to exporting firms established after 1980.

The decision to join the European monetary system and break away from parity with sterling was a mixed blessing for many Irish firms. The government's control over devaluation was reduced while high rates of domestic inflation reduced the competitiveness of Irish exports. If it were not for the rise in the value of sterling after 1979 manufacturing firms exporting to the British market would have been severely hit.

A EUROPEAN COMPANY?

The Community affects industry in other ways than providing a market for its products or stabilising exchange rates. As part of its attempt to create a unified market, the Commission has attempted to develop a unified code of company law which would govern the operation of firms, facilitating investment in other member states, standardising accounting practices and encouraging mergers. The Community's first company law directive (68/151) was adopted by the Council of Ministers in 1968. It lays down basic legal requirements for registered companies in member states. It provides for the setting up of company registers and places an obligation on all firms to publish information about their subscribed capital, annual accounts, the names of directors and company statutes. The second directive was adopted in 1976 and it lays down harmonised standards for the formation and maintenance of capital of public limited companies to protect the interests of shareholders and creditors. The directive was to have been implemented in all member states by January 1979 but four member states including Ireland failed to meet the deadline. In October 1982 Ireland was condemned by the European Court for failing to comply. The directive was eventually implemented by the Company (Amendment) Act 1983.

The third directive (78/855) facilitates mergers between companies in the same member state while protecting the interests of shareholders, creditors, employees and debenture holders. The original deadline for implementing the directive was October 1981 but the Commission has extended it to January 1986 so that it can be implemented with the sixth directive covering companies going into liquidation. The fourth directive (78/660) lays down basic rules for a harmonised system of accounting and reporting by companies throughout the EEC. It applies to all public and private limited liability companies apart from credit institutions and insurance companies, while small firms are given certain concessions. The terms of this directive have not been implemented, the deadline of January 1982 having been ignored. The proposed fifth directive is a highly controversial measure which is mainly concerned with the structure and administration of public limited liability companies. Agreement on it has been held up since 1972 because of opposition to worker participation in the decision-making structure of companies. The Commission originally proposed a system which would have given companies no choice as to how they would organise worker participation but in 1982 they revised their proposal to limit the requirement to firms with more than 1,000 workers and to allow firms to choose from four alternative forms of employee participation. The proposed directive has already had some impact on this country. The Worker Participation (State Enterprises) Act, 1976 provides for worker participation on the boards of seven state-sponsored companies. Member states have until January 1986 to implement the directive.

The Commission has a number of other proposals up its sleeve for standardising the practice of companies, including banks and insurance companies. The one that has generated more opposition from EEC and US industry than any previous proposal on company law is the proposed 'Vredeling' directive from the Social Affairs DG of the Commission on procedures for informing and consulting the employees of multinational companies. If passed, these firms would have to inform their workers at regular intervals of the overall operations of both the individual company and of the group of companies to which it belongs. Management would also have to consult with employee representatives on decisions taken by the parent company - whether in the EEC or not - likely to have a substantial effect on employees within the Community. While the proposal is strongly supported by the trade union movement in the Community, industrialists fear that the directive would force them to divulge sensitive business secrets thus doing harm to their competitiveness. Some multinationals have threatened to withdraw investment from the Community if too many obligations are placed upon them.

Concern with workers' rights has been a constant theme of the

Community's approach to company law. An important directive (77/187), also from the Social Affairs DG, aims at protecting workers' rights when their company merges with or is transferred to another company. It provides for the transfer of existing rights and obligations to the new employer and outlaws the dismissal of employees as a direct consequence of a simple merger or transfer. A further directive on mass dismissals (75/129) lays down procedures for informing and consulting staff when a firm intends to make a proportion of the workforce redundant.

It is hoped that by making it easier for companies in different member states to merge or to expand from one state into another European firms will be able to take advantage of the economies of scale offered by the size of the Community market. Traditionally restricted by national barriers, service industries have benefited most from EEC rules. Irish banks, insurance companies, real estate and law firms, and haulage companies can now establish themselves in other member states. The small size of the Irish market makes it less attractive to EEC firms to set up in Ireland. The European Business Centre, better known as the 'Marriage Bureau' in Brussels encourages small and medium-sized firms to link up with similar firms in other Community countries. The Joint Ventures Department of the Industrial Development Authority, in liaison with the Business Centre, acts as a 'marriage broker', bringing together overseas and Irish firms with similar interests. A computerised system of information on Community markets, called Euronet, is available to anyone with access to a suitable terminal linked to the telephone network. The charge for the service is based on time, not distance, so that users from Dublin, Copenhagen and Brussels pay the same price.

The results of these measures have so far not been impressive with only thirty Irish firms establishing contact with opposite numbers in other member states. Because of the small size of the Irish home market and the small size of firms, Irish enterprises have difficulty in achieving the economies of scale available to larger firms in other parts of the EEC.

According to Paddy Jordan of the Confederation of Irish Industry, the inability of Irish marketing executives to speak continental languages has led to over-reliance on the British market. 'We have made,' he says, 'some impact in Belgium and Holland, but that's because business people there speak English. If Ireland were to export as much proportionately in France and Germany as we do to the Dutch and Belgians, our balance of trade deficit would be eliminated overnight.' This cultural limitation may explain why many successful Irish firms, when seeking to invest or diversify abroad, have done so in the United States.

Customs duties and company law are not the only barriers to intra-Community trade. Different standards of measurement and weight, requirements for packaging and labelling, specifications on ingredients of products and rules to ensure the safety of products can all be used as reasons why a member state restricts the free circulation of goods from another member. The Commission has pursued a policy of requiring member states to harmonise these non-tariff barriers to trade. The effect has been to ensure the Communitywide circulation of vehicles, machinery, electrical equipment, measuring instruments, pharmaceutical products and processed food. The fervour of the Commission aroused a good deal of opposition and ridicule in the mid-1970s. Rumours of a common Euro-bread and Euro-beer gave the Commission a bad press. It led to speculation that the Community was about to harmonise nursery rhymes and even birth rates! Since then the Commission has modified its approach to one requiring goods which circulate freely in the Community to respect minimum norms, while allowing producers to cater for the special taste of their domestic market.

THE FUTURE

European industry has major problems to resolve if it is to regain markets lost in the last decade to its chief competitors, Japan and the US. The Commission would like to tackle the declining competitiveness of Community industry on a broad front. Much investment has been made in developing energy sources other than oil to reduce the Community's import bill. It was in this context that large loans were provided for the ESB's new coal-generating plant at Moneypoint, Co. Clare, and for laying the natural gas pipeline from Cork to Dublin. The Commission would also like to see much greater attention given to research and development in European firms and to the encouragement of innovation, on the assumption that the great industrial battles over telematics and biotechnology can only be waged at world level.

It would also like to see a reversal of the trend towards public-sector intervention in the management of firms. Any measures the Commission might take in this area could conflict with the approach of the Irish government. An influential report from the National Economic and Social Council by the Telesis consultancy group pointed out that the flow of foreign investment to Ireland in recent years shows signs of diminishing and that with the enlargement of the Community to include Spain and Portugal it will be even more difficult to attract such investment to this country. They recommend a restructuring of tax and grant incentives to encourage indigenous firms to develop products of the future and that the government itself should take the initiative in forming new large companies to lead an export drive.

If Irish industry, whether public or private, is to survive it must be able to sell its products competitively on Community and world markets. The high level of inflation, fuelled by demands for increased wages unmatched by increases in productivity, is making it difficult to sell goods abroad. Economist Alan Matthews has pointed out that the rise in living standards during the past decade was not due to an increase in the productive base of the economy but was built initially on transfers from the EEC and subsequently by recourse to foreign borrowing. It remains as important as it was in the early 1960s to adapt Irish society to the disciplines of free trade in a small open economy.

BOOM, BABY, BOOM

The EEC is running out of children. The most worried country is France, where the birth rate is well below the EEC average. So the two French commissioners in Brussels are enthusiastically backing a new directive proposed by the Dutch social affairs commissioner, Mr Henk Vredeling, to raise birth rates and to harmonise legislation on fertility. The directive would oblige all member states to introduce incentives to increase birth rates. Controversially, the EEC wants to impose a Community-wide tax of 15% on the cost of all contraceptives sold in the Nine and use the revenue for an education programme on the advantages of having more babies. A second aim is to harmonise the wide variation in birth rates within the Community. Ireland, for example, has a birth rate of 21.5 per 1,000, twice the EEC average. If the directive is adopted, Ireland will have to run a pilot surveillance scheme of married men's behaviour in their leisure hours - backed up, if necessary, by a system of baby licensing. Irish officials have reacted angrily, calling the scheme 'just harmonisation for harmonisation's sake'.
                                                            The Economist, 1 April 1978

111

13
Trade

Thanks to agriculture, Ireland maintains a healthy balance of trade with most of its EEC partners.

THE COMMUNITY IS the largest trading bloc in the world, accounting in 1982 for 19% of trade compared to 14% for the US and 8% for Japan. In the present recession, however, pressures have grown for protectionist measures that threaten the open trading system favoured by the Community, straining relations between the Community and its main partners, the US and Japan. There has not been a return to beggar-my-neighbour policies of the 1930s but 'managed trade' has become more widespread as governments face public demands to safeguard jobs.

More than to the US or Japan, external trade is important to the Community, amounting to a quarter of the gross domestic product (GDP) of the ten EEC states. After Belgium/Luxembourg, Ireland is the most trade-dependent EEC country at about 55% of GDP. France and Greece are the two states least dependent on trade at about 20% of GDP. About 51%

112

of Community trade took place in 1982 among the Ten, compared to 35% among the Six in 1958. This growth resulted from the abolition of customs duties and quantitative restrictions within the common market.

The common external tariff makes the Community a single trading entity. Indeed, Article 113.3 of the Treaty empowers the Commission to negotiate on behalf of the Community at international fora dealing with trade. The member states meet beforehand to work out a negotiating mandate for the Commission and they endorse the final settlement. In particular, the Commission represents the Community at the General Agreement on Tariffs and Trade (GATT) which was set up in 1948 and is composed of eighty-eight governments representing four-fifths of world trade. In the Dillon GATT round (1960-62) Community tariffs were lowered by about 8%; in the Kennedy round (1964-67) by 35% to 40%, and in the Tokyo round (1973-79) they are to be reduced from 9% to 7.5% by 1988. The Community exports more than it imports except with the US and countries in Northern Europe.

RELATIONS WITH OTHER COUNTRIES

United States The US was an enthusiastic advocate of European union but its enthusiasm waned in the economic sphere as the Community threatened the US share of world trade. The Community is the US's best customer taking 23% of US exports and accounting for 17% of its imports. The US has enjoyed a consistent and substantial trade surplus with the Community, mainly from engineering products and farm goods. In agriculture alone the Community imported $9 billion of farm goods from the US in 1981 while exporting only $2 billion worth to the US. The Reagan administration has intensified its attack on the EEC's farm policy, especially its export subsidies, which it sees as an obstacle to US farmers gaining a bigger share of world markets. The Community fears that the US might dump dairy stocks on the world market at reduced prices.

A particular instance of market rivalry was a US decision to sell cut-price wheat flour to Egypt, an EEC customer. Washington has threatened to retaliate if US soyabean-oil sales are affected by the introduction by the EEC of a tax on vegetable oils and livestock-feed ingredients.

In 1982 the Community successfully resisted US pressure to penalise European subsidiaries of US corporations for supplying the Soviet Union with materials for a gas pipeline from Siberia. Another source of friction was partly resolved in October 1980 when Industry Commissioner Etienne Davignon negotiated a voluntary restraint agreement limiting EEC steel exports to the US. This did not stop the US from imposing restrictions on special steel imports. High US interest rates have hindered European recovery and investment and dampened world trade.

Japan With a population of 116 million Japan is the third pillar of the free trading system, but relations with the Community have been even more strained than between the Community and the US because the Japanese market is so difficult to penetrate. Even though Japanese industry is not protected by higher customs duties than US industry, it is difficult for European - and US - businesses to sell their goods in Japan on account of language difficulties and non-tariff restrictions. The Community accounts for only 5.5% of Japanese imports but takes 12.5% of its exports, mainly in sensitive sectors. The Community's massive trade deficit with Japan has grown twenty-fold since 1970 and stood at about IR£7.5 billion in 1982. The Council of Ministers has reacted by setting up a surveillance system to monitor imports of Japanese cars, colour TV sets and tubes and numerically controlled machine tools. In response to Community complaints the Japanese have agreed to moderate some of their exports and to open up their market to Community goods, but so far with little effect.

Mediterranean Countries The Community has a number of special agreements with countries in the Mediterranean basin signed during the 1960s and renewed in 1972. Turkey, Cyprus and Malta have signed association agreements which aim to progressively create a customs union with the Community. The Maghreb countries (Algeria, Morocco and Tunisia) and the Mashreq countries (Egypt, Jordan, Lebanon and Syria), together with Israel and Yugoslavia, signed agreements providing for commercial, industrial, technical and financial cooperation with the Community but which do not involve the creation of a full customs union. All these agreements in theory give the countries concerned customs-free access to the Community for industrial goods and for some agricultural products and make financial aid available. The recession of the 1970s put the principle of free access to Community markets to the test. Many goods which the Mediterranean countries wished to export to the Community, such as steel and textiles, were the same ones which were under threat in member states. The Community imposed import restrictions on goods coming from these countries thereby contributing to a doubling of the trade deficit in favour of the Community between 1973 and 1980. The Mediterranean countries in turn have reduced their imports of Community products because they cannot afford to pay for them. The creation of a more liberal and balanced relationship with the Mediterranean countries is a major item on the Community's agenda for the 1980s.

European Free Trade Association (EFTA) On 1 January 1984 the Community and the EFTA agreed on free circulation of industrial goods. This completed a process of removing tariff barriers and quantitative restrictions on industrial products that began in 1972 when the Community signed a free trade agreement with Austria, Iceland, Sweden and Switzerland and later with Norway, Finland and Portugal. Britain and Denmark, but not Ireland, had been EFTA members before joining the Community in 1973.

With 312 million consumers between them the EEC and EFTA form the largest free trade area for industrial products in the world. The Community has developed a network of cooperation with EFTA greater than with any other industrial partner, exchanging information on consumer protection, the environment, telecommunications, economic and monetary policy, health and safety at work, energy, transport, development and industrial policy, as well as joint participation in science and technology programmes. In the 1980s the Community hopes to promote trade in agricultural products.

Soviet Union and Eastern Europe Trade between the Community and countries of the Eastern bloc is complicated by the refusal of the Soviet Union to officially recognise the Community. The Community sells only 10% of its goods to the Eastern bloc countries. In 1980 the Community signed a non-preferential trade agreement with Romania covering industrial goods. A cooperation agreement was signed in April 1980 with Yugoslavia allowing it tariff-free imports. More recently, Hungary and Bulgaria have shown an interest in expanding commercial ties with EEC countries.

Australia and New Zealand Irish and French farmers complain about the supplies of meat and dairy products from these two commonwealth countries to the British market despite the surplus of such products in the Community. If, however, the Community reduced or abolished these imports, large amounts of dairy products could be dumped by New Zealand on the world market. The Commission wants to gradually reduce imports of New Zealand butter from its present 87,000 tonnes a year to 75,000 tonnes by 1988.

People's Republic of China The first trade link between Ireland and China was in 1978 when the Community signed a non-preferential trade agreement with China. This was the first trade agreement between the Community and a state-trading country. China was granted the 'most favoured nation' status by the Community and China said it would give favourable consideration to EEC imports. During a six-day visit to China in November 1983 Commission President Gaston Thorn announced a grant of £4.5 millon to help China develop its agricultural and food-processing technology. This was the first grant made to China under the Community's financial and technical assistance programme for non-associated developing countries.

Latin America The five members of the ANDEAN PACT - Bolivia, Colombia, Equador, Peru and Venezuela - concluded a five-year agreement for trade and cooperation with the Community in December 1983. Trade and industrial cooperation between the two regions should increase as European investment in the ANDEAN countries rises. This signing improved Europe's relations with Latin America following Argentina's conflict with Britain over the Falklands. There are plans to open a Europe/Latin American Institute of Studies.

Central America US involvement in this region has alarmed European opinion, especially after the murder of Archbishop Romero in El Salvador in 1980. The European Councils in March and June 1982 called for reforms to ease tensions. This led to a decision by the Council of Ministers to allocate about IR£20 million in 1982 for agricultural reform programmes in Nicaragua, Costa Rica, Honduras and the Dominican Republic.

The Gulf States The Community is a major trade partner of the Gulf States of Bahrain, Iraq, Kuwait, Oman, Qatar, Saudi Arabia and the United Arab Emirates. With about 30% of the world's production of crude oil the Gulf States provide an important source for the Community's energy imports. Their share of EEC exports rose from 1.6% in 1973 to 6.5% in 1978. About 89% of these exports in 1978 were manufactured goods, particularly machinery and transport equipment. Despite the importance of this region, the Community has not entered into contractual economic relations with it, similar, for instance, to the diplomatic and economic links with other Arab countries - Sudan, Mauritania, Djibouti and Somalia - in the Lomé Convention.

Asean In 1972 the ASEAN countries - Indonesia, Malaysia, the Philippines, Singapore and Thailand - signed a non-preferential cooperation agreement with the Community.

IRISH TRADE AND THE EEC

Membership of the Community has greatly altered the pattern of Irish trade, particularly exports. In the early 1970s agricultural exports accounted for 42% of exports, of which 70% were sold to the UK and only 17% to continental EEC countries. By 1981 the UK share of food exports was 45% while the other member states took 30%. Being in the Community

116

Table 6

The Community's Most Important Trading Partners in 1982

IMPORTS			EXPORTS		
RANK		% OF TOTAL	RANK		% OF TOTAL
1	USA	16.7	1	USA	15.0
2	Saudi Arabia	8.1	2	Switzerland	8.0
3	Japan	5.6	3	Sweden	4.9
4	Switzerland	5.4	4	Saudi Arabia	4.5
5	USSR	5.3	5	Austria	4.4
6	Sweden	4.1	6	Spain	3.6
7	Norway	3.5	7	USSR	3.1
8	Spain	3.2	8	Iraq	3.1
9	Libya	2.8	9	Norway	2.4
10	Algeria	2.7	10	Nigeria	2.4
11	Austria	2.7	11	South Africa	2.3
12	South Africa	2.3	12	Japan	2.2
13	Iran	2.2	13	Algeria	1.9
14	Canada	2.0	14	Libya	1.7
15	Nigeria	2.0	15	Australia	1.6
16	Brazil	1.9	16	Canada	1.6
17	Finland	1.6	17	Egypt	1.5
18	Hong Kong	1.2	18	Finland	1.5
19	UAE (United Arab Emirates)	1.2	19	Yugoslavia	1.5
20	Australia	0.9	20	India	1.4
Share of 20 partners in total Extra-EEC Imports		75.4	Share of 20 partners in total Extra-EEC Exports		68.6

Source: Monthly External Trade Bulletins, EUROSTAT

117

was a vital factor in attracting foreign firms to this country; these firms have since become leading exporters of manufacturing goods. The EEC has also helped Ireland to develop trade with the rest of the world, with exports to non-EEC countries now accounting for about the same share of Irish exports as EEC member states. About 8% of Irish exports go to the US, while less developed countries such as Libya, Nigeria, Mexico, Egypt and Iran are becoming important markets for Irish goods, particularly food products and live animals. The EEC is directly involved in these agricultural exports since most are exported with subsidies from the common agricultural policy. Furthermore, as a member of the EEC Ireland has benefited from the many trading arrangements negotiated by the Community which ensure that Irish products cannot be excluded from a market at the whim of the country concerned.

PROSPECTS

A 1983 Commission publication on the external trade situation showed that the Community imports almost half of its energy needs and about three-quarters of other vital raw materials. Thus to maintain living standards the Community must export finished products. It also needs to become more competitive. Between 1958 and 1972 the volume of world trade tripled but in the next decade it rose by only half, actually shrinking slightly in 1981 and 1982. 'Community trade with the rest of the world followed more or less the same pattern,' reported the Commission. 'European imports and exports increased 13 times in value between 1958 and 1982, slightly below the rate for world trade as a whole. During this period, however, the shares in world trade of the Community (about 23% in 1958) and the United States have been eroded by the growing economic power of Japan, the oil-producing countries and newly industrialised countries in Asia.'

14
Political Cooperation

Garret FitzGerald, Jack Lynch, Liam Cosgrave and Richard Burke return from the twenty-fifth anniversary celebrations of the EEC.

A GROUP OF EEC correspondents were guests in The Hague of the Dutch government which was due to take over the Community presidency for the first half of 1981. While they were there a report in *Le Monde* newspaper caught their attention. President Giscard d'Estaing of France had disclosed that at a recent European Council in Luxembourg there had been a row among the heads of state and government over the 'neutralist' remarks of one of the leaders in regard to public dislike of the NATO decision to deploy US medium-range missiles in western Europe. Who was this neutralist? asked *Le Monde*. Was it Denmark's Anker Joergensen? Holland's Andries Van Agt? Or perhaps the prime minister of neutral Ireland, Charles Haughey? A few hours later the journalists eagerly surrounded Mr Van Agt at Government Buildings. Standing beneath a portrait of William of Orange - himself no neutral at the Battle of the Boyne - Mr Van Agt appeared to be ill at ease but seemed determined to clear himself of suspicion and was ready to let it be known discreetly that the bad boy of the European Council resided in Copenhagen, not The Hague. One of the journalists, John Cooney of *The Irish Times*, asked Mr. Van Agt whether all the government leaders were present for the conversation about the Euromissiles. 'Of course,' smiled Mr Van Agt. 'Was Mr Haughey of Ireland present?' Cooney asked. 'Yes,' said a puzzled Van Agt. 'Why do you ask such a question . . .', he began as an official leaned over him and whispered to him that Ireland is not a NATO member. Oh!

Oh indeed, reacts the public in Ireland on hearing of such instances of overlapping between the concerns of the European Community and the activities of NATO.

Joining the EEC gave Ireland the opportunity to develop foreign policies on a wide range of issues with its partners and to have a view - even an influence - on world events. At the same time Ireland was committing itself to seeking common ground with partners of whom all are members of NATO although France is not a member of the NATO command.

The discussion on the deployment of US missiles among the EEC leaders took place under the heading of 'political cooperation', the name given to the attempt by the member states to coordinate their foreign policies. Since defence and security vitally affect the foreign policies of our partners, it is not surprising that a lot of discussion under the heading of political cooperation takes place on these issues. Political cooperation is seen by all member states as an important step on the road to a political union.

STRUCTURES

The coordination of the foreign policies of the member states was in operation prior to Ireland's joining in 1973, but this was the least-known part of the Community's work. The Hague summit in December 1969 which favoured admitting new members, including Ireland, instructed the foreign ministers of the Six to study 'the best way of achieving progress in the matter of political unification within the context of enlargement'. In charge of preparations was a Belgian diplomat, Etienne Davignon, later a commissioner, and his report, which was approved in Luxembourg in October 1970, stated that 'efforts ought first to concentrate specifically on the coordination of foreign policies in order to show the whole world that Europe has a political mission'.

The Luxembourg report set up the machinery for European political cooperation (EPC - or POCO as it is called by officials). Foreign ministers would meet twice a year, quite separately from their meetings as the Council of Ministers and at a separate venue. (This led to the absurd situation in 1973 when a political cooperation meeting was held in Copenhagen and the same ministers then flew to Brussels to meet as the Council of Ministers!) A political committee of senior diplomats from the foreign ministries would also meet four times a year to prepare the ministerial meetings and carry out any tasks delegated to them by the ministers.

The Commission, however, was given no role in proposing policies or administering the decisions of the foreign ministers. The task of organising and servicing meetings of EPC falls to the foreign ministry of the member state which holds the presidency of the EEC.

For the most part operating out of the public eye, EPC has been a growth area in EEC partnership. It is a 'closed door' system of diplomacy which is conducted by the ten foreign ministries outside the legal restraints of the Community and away from the Commission, though the Commission is represented at meetings. A group of correspondents was set up to assist the political directors (the senior diplomats). That group was to implement political cooperation decisions and to prepare meetings of the political directors on the basis of instructions from them.

An EEC intelligence network has grown up: telex messages flood daily into each of the foreign ministries. Coded telegrams, known as COREU (Correspondance Européenne), do the rounds of the EEC capitals. Provision was made for working parties from the foreign ministries to meet on specific subjects. The embassies of the Ten work together in the implementation of political cooperation, especially in publishing statements by the foreign ministers. Ambassadors of the Community resident in non-EEC countries, including Moscow, meet regularly to coordinate their views and share information. Ambassadors of EEC countries attached to international organisations, such as the United Nations, regularly seek common positions on important questions dealt with by those organisations.

Agreed positions have been taken up on a wide range of international questions including the Middle East, Cyprus, Portugal, the Conference on Security and Disarmament, on Namibia, on international terrorism, on Zimbabwe, against apartheid in South Africa, against the Russian 'intervention' in Afghanistan, against the occupation of the American embassy in Iran, in support of Solidarity in Poland and against the Argentine invasion of the Falklands.

NEUTRALITY

There is an inherent conflict between Ireland's membership of the EEC and the maintenance of neutrality. The EEC is committed to the long-term goal of political union, which in the eyes of many will involve some form of military commitment. The Treaty of Rome contains provisions which conflict with the legal requirement that neutral states treat belligerents impartially in any conflict. Article 224 for example, provides for the continuation of Community policies in time of war, permitting the Council of Ministers to prohibit exports or imports from particular countries. Such countries might well be combatants in a war. Austria, Sweden and Switzerland considered that this Article and the proposed extension of majority voting in the Council of Ministers precluded them, as neutral countries, from joining the EEC.

The question of whether Ireland's neutrality is compatible with EEC membership has never been resolved. In the early 1960s when Ireland first considered joining the EEC, Sean Lemass could maintain on the one hand that the EEC had no military links and obligations but on the other hand recognise that 'a military commitment will be an inevitable consequence of our joining the Common Market and ultimately we would be prepared to yield even the technical label of neutrality. We are prepared to go into this integrated Europe without any reservation as to how far this will take us in the field of foreign policy and defence.' (*New York Times*, 18 July 1962). Nor was Sean MacBride's reason for not joining NATO in 1949 - the continued British occupation of Northern Ireland - seen as an obstacle to partnership with Britain in the EEC.

The 1972 White Paper on EEC membership stated the government's readiness to work with the other member states for political unification in Europe. But is also emphasised that the Treaties of Rome and Paris did 'not entail any military or defence commitments and no such commitments are involved in Ireland's acceptance of these Treaties'.

Foreign Minister Patrick Hillery did not dismiss the possibility of a future European defence involvement by Ireland, repeating the view of Lemass that as part of a united Europe Ireland would play its part in defending that Community. Thus, Dr Hillery's successor Garret FitzGerald could endorse a document on European identity published in Copenhagen in December 1973, a key passage of which stated: 'The Nine, one of whose essential aims is to maintain peace, will never succeed in doing so if they neglect their own security. Those of them who are members of the Atlantic Alliance consider that in the present circumstances there is no alternative to the security provided by the nuclear weapons of the United States and by the presence of North American forces in Europe; and they agree that in the light of the relative military vulnerability of Europe, the Europeans should, if they wish to preserve their independence, hold to their commitments and make constant efforts to ensure that they have adequate means of defence at their disposal.'

There has been no pressure from outside for Ireland to join NATO. Indeed Irish non-membership of NATO was cited by Dr FitzGerald as an asset for the Community, instancing the visit which he made to Portugal as Community president in 1975 shortly after the revolution there. With feelings high against NATO in Lisbon, an Irish EEC president was welcomed as a bona fide spokesman.

But since 1979, the year of the decision to deploy American missiles in Europe and the intervention of the Soviet Union in Afghanistan, security has been uppermost in the minds of western European leaders. So it is not surprising that during European Council sessions the opportunity has been taken on occasion by them to exchange views on East-West balance of power matters. One such instance was at Dublin Castle in November 1979 when under the presidency of Jack Lynch they discussed the deployment of the Cruise and Pershing missiles.

In 1981 suggestions were made by some member states that political cooperation might be expanded to include discussion of the military security of Western Europe. The Irish government considered that such talks would impinge on Ireland's neutrality and in the autumn of 1981, Irish diplomats won a guarantee from the nine partners that political cooperation would cover only the 'political aspects of security' such as disarmament and confidence-building measures. This, argued Professor Jim Dooge, Minister for Foreign Affairs, took account of Ireland's position by excluding discussion of defence questions appropriate to a military alliance. In Ireland's view this formally and publicly stated what had already been the situation.

The question of neutrality also arises in the context of economic sanctions against combatants. Ireland has been party to EEC decisions which demonstrate that in the EEC it is not possible to be strictly neutral. Faced with difficult choices in the working out of Community responses to certain world crises, Ireland took its political solidarity with the West a stage further into the trade areas by backing economic sanctions against the Soviet Union over Afghanistan and Poland and against Iran over the holding of American diplomats hostage.

The underlying tension between neutrality and membership surfaced sharply in 1982 when the Taoiseach, Mr Haughey, withdrew Irish support for EEC sanctions against Argentina after the sinking of the *Belgrano* outside UK territorial waters on the grounds that he was upholding 'Ireland's traditional role of neutrality in relation to armed conflicts'. This decision was seen by Dennis Kennedy of *The Irish Times* as an extension of the meaning of Irish neutrality; a maximalist interpretation of it similar to the views of the Labour Party, the Workers' Party and the Irish Sovereignty Movement, among others, who would prefer Ireland to join the non-aligned group of countries or be strictly neutral like Switzerland, Austria or Sweden.

The Community has made little advance towards political union. No major war has broken out since the EEC was founded and majority voting is rarely used. Therefore membership of the Community has not yet posed a hard choice for the Irish between the aspiration of neutrality and the reality of economic benefit. The question is whether, if it came to the crunch, Ireland would give up its membership of the Community to maintain its solitary stance on neutrality.

. . . experience has taught me that it is not a good thing for the British to obtain special conditions and an exceptional position in their relationships with others, or even for them to cherish such hopes. On the other hand, they are at their best if you firmly offer to work with them on an equal footing. If you stick to your principles, there is every likelihood that the British will sooner or later adapt to the situation and become partners in the full sense of the word.   Jean Monnet, *Memoirs*

A country that has taken so few steps to nurture intellectual traditions can scarcely be expected to produce sustained serious contributions towards European thought. Lachrymose invocations of those intrepid pioneers on the Berlaymont trail, St Columba and St Gall, do not suffice to close the gap.

Joseph Lee, *Reflections on Ireland in the EEC*, ICEM, 1984

15
The Community and the Third World

Garret FitzGerald, as President of the EEC, at the signing of the first Lomé Convention, 1975.

MOTIVATED BY enlightened self interest and humanitarianism the Community has developed a sophisticated relationship with many Third World countries. Arising from historical ties with former colonies in Africa, the Community has progressed towards a relationship with the Third World based on partnership and economic interdependence. While the creation of a just economic order may seem as far away as ever, the Community does more than the US, the Soviet bloc or Japan to shift the balance in favour of the developing world.

By the early 1970s the Community had become the largest trading bloc in the world. Its economic might and the colonial past of most of its members meant that it could not ignore the demand from the newly independent countries for a more equitable share of world trade. In 1971 the Community pioneered a generalised scheme of preferences (GSP)

125

which reduced import duties on manufacturing goods entering the common market from developing countries. By 1981 the GSP covered three hundred processed agricultural goods and all industrial goods coming from a hundred developing countries.

The Community is more dependent on raw materials from developing countries than either the US or the Soviet Union. In the early 1970s nine out of ten tonnes of oil consumed in the Community originated in the Third World. As the Community also depends heavily on the Third World for tea, coffee, cotton, teak, bananas, iron ore, bauxite, copper and tin, manganese, phosphate and vegetable oils, it made sense for the Community to establish good relations to ensure continuing supplies of these products. It was also clear in the 1970s that the Third World was becoming the single biggest market for Community products and the market which was expanding at the fastest rate. In 1977, 37% of Community exports went to developing countries compared with 12% to the US and 22% to countries in northern Europe. If developing countries were unable to expand their economies they could not afford to pay for the goods which the member states excelled in producing — engineering products for machines and for transport and communications.

In 1971 the Commission initiated debate within the Community on a development cooperation policy. The 1972 Paris summit meeting gave the Community a very wide mandate to act, despite the absence of Treaty provisions. A new policy was given added urgency with the accession of Britain to the Community. Britain's commitments to developing countries through the commonwealth were much greater than any of the existing member states. During negotiations on accession, the British insisted that the Community extend a special relationship to developing commonwealth countries to compensate them for the loss of benefits under the commonwealth preference system. When the 1963 Yaoundé convention, with eighteen African countries (mainly former French colonies), expired in 1975 it was replaced by a convention covering many more developing countries and introducing a new spirit of partnership and interdependence to trade relations between the Community and the Third World. Commonwealth countries India and Bangladesh were excluded because their size and poverty would have meant spreading Community aid too thinly.

The new convention was signed in Lomé, the capital of Togo, in 1975 on behalf of the Community and forty-six African, Caribbean and Pacific states (ACP). Garret FitzGerald, EEC President in office, signed the convention on behalf of the Community, describing it as a model of the economic relations which should exist between the industrial and the developing world. Under the terms of the convention, renewed in 1980 for a further five years and extended to include sixty ACP countries, customs duties and quantitative restrictions have been eliminated on industrial and most agricultural exports from the ACP countries to the EEC. Products covered by the common agricultural policy are excluded. A major innovation is that the ACP countries are not required to grant preferential customs treatment to Community exports. They must, however, treat Community products at least as favourably as products from any other trading partner.

The most radical change introduced under the convention is the system of stabilisation of export earnings (STABEX). One of the major problems facing countries dependent on the export earnings from raw materials is the fluctuation in prices from year to year. Too much rain or too little can destroy crops and wipe out a country's ability to pay for imports or service foreign debts. Since production of many of these products is planned years in advance it is not possible to respond quickly to sudden changes in demand as in highly industrialised economies. In the negotiations on the convention the Commission proposed a mechanism for stabilising the price of certain raw materials.

The STABEX system works as a sort of international social security scheme protecting countries which depend on sales of their agricultural product against bad years and compensating them for instability resulting from the play of free market forces. If the export receipts of any ACP country from any of the forty-four products covered by the scheme falls by more than a certain percentage below an agreed reference price, the European development fund will provide compensation which the better off ACP countries are expected to refund when the market improves. STABEX applies mainly to agricultural goods such as cocoa, coffee, peanuts, tea and sisal but the second convention added certain minerals to the list. The advantage of the system to the consumer in the Community is that the supply and the price of these products is more stable than before.

Probably no other agreement defined in such detail ways in which the developed and developing countries could cooperate on industrial affairs as the first Lomé convention. Unfortunately, the ambitious expections were not fulfilled and the second convention is more precise in the cooperation goals to be achieved. Particular emphasis is paid to helping ACP countries develop alternative sources of energy to imported oil and to increased food production by improving the rural infrastructure. The European development fund and the European Investment Bank provide assistance for investment in projects to achieve these aims and to encourage the transfer of appropriate technology and improved marketing of ACP products. The Joint Centre for Industrial Development and the Centre for Technical, Agricultural and Rural Cooperation provide technical expertise and incentives for development projects in ACP countries.

Unlike most trade arrangements between the industrial and developed world, the convention has an elaborate institutional framework for economic cooperation. The operation of the convention is overseen by a council of ministers, which includes representatives of the Commission, the member states of the EEC and a representative from each of the ACP states. It meets once a year and its decisions are binding on the contracting parties. The council is assisted by a committee of ambassadors which is responsible for the day-to-day operation of the convention. There is also a consultative assembly made up of equal numbers of members of the European Parliament and delegates from the ACP states. The European development fund provides the finance for STABEX and development cooperation under the convention.

Ireland's contribution to the European development fund under the second convention is IR£13 million out of a total fund of IR£3 billion. Irish firms are entitled to compete for cooperation projects which are advertised for international tender in the Commission's journal *EEC-ACP Courier*. Irish state-sponsored companies have been particularly successful in winning contracts for consultancy work and technical assistance, worth IR£5.8 million by March 1983. Córas Tráchtála won the largest technical cooperation contract awarded under the fund, designed to improve the marketing of products in Caribbean countries. In 1982 it was asked to take on the job of evaluating the effectiveness of the second Lomé convention.

Irish firms have won contracts to supply IR£3.4 million worth of goods under contracts for equipment and pesticides. Commissioner Burke has pointed out, however, that Irish firms have shown little interest in competing for construction, telecommunications, infrastructure or irrigation projects sponsored by the European development fund, although 60% of funds are earmarked for these projects.

Despite expectations, guaranteed free access for ACP products to the Community market has produced few results. The performance of the ACPs since 1975 is lower than the average for all developing countries and their share of exports in world trade has fallen by comparison with that of other Third World countries. The STABEX system which worked well under the first convention, has proved inadequate for conditions in the 1980s. In 1981 disbursements met about half the claims submitted and in 1982 only 40%. Slack markets for raw materials have lessened the concern of member states about security of supply.

There may be a shift of emphasis in the convention to replace the second Lomé agreement. Mr Pisani, the commissioner responsible for Third World affairs, has published a blueprint for a new convention which would increase the role of aid at the expense of trade. The commissioner would like to stimulate grassroots development by means of a multitude of small-scale practical schemes, particularly in the countryside, that would meet the real needs of people. There would be less emphasis on individual projects and more on programmes to increase food production. ACP countries would be obliged to use receipts from the STABEX system towards these programmes. The ACPs dislike the idea of assistance being tied in any way or of monitoring by the Community. However, Pisani's scheme is likely to be considered too generous by the UK and West Germany who are reluctant to increase their commitments to Third World development.

FOOD AID

Since 1968 the Community has distributed food to countries with famines or food shortages. During the 1970s the world food situation became increasingly serious. Climatic changes brought prolonged drought to parts of Africa and Asia. Oil-price rises increased the cost of fertiliser and pesticides and of using farm machinery. Meanwhile the population of the Third World expanded, and is still expanding, at an alarming rate. Forty years ago Asia, Africa and Latin America were net exporters of basic foodstuffs but are now dependent on imports. Africa produces 9% less food per head of its population than it did ten years ago.

In response to criticisms from the European Parliament that Community food aid was too dependent on the level of agricultural surpluses in the Community, member states agreed in 1981 to implement an action plan against world hunger which aims to improve agricultural production and nutrition in developing countries as well as responding to emergency calls for food aid. Food aid and development cooperation are to be more closely allied to assist countries improve their food production over a number of years. Helping the Third World feed itself makes good economic sense for the EEC. If developing countries have to spend their hard-won export earnings on food, they will have no money to buy products manufactured in Europe and member states' economies will suffer. Many developing countries already spend 20% of their foreign currency on food imports.

BEYOND THE ACP

In addition to the special relationship with the ACP countries the Community has preferential trade agreements with developing countries in Asia and South America.

Within the framework of the United Nations, EEC member states have participated in the North-South Dialogue, the name given to wide-ranging discussions begun in the 1970s on the many imbalances between the industrialised countries, mainly in the northern hemisphere, and the developing world in the southern hemisphere. The Community, whose economic power is not matched by military or political muscle, has attempted to play the role of the honest broker in relations between the Third World and the other large trading blocs. The objectives of the Dialogue have been underlined by the work of the North-South Commission chaired by Willy Brandt, former West German Chancellor. In two major reports the Commission has pointed to the growing crisis in the Third World and to the illogicality of increasing the production of armaments while millions are on the brink of starvation. The work of the Commission has not had much immediate impact on the North-South Dialogue which has almost disappeared from the agenda of the United Nations. Speaking in October 1983 of the need to give priority to North-South problems Jim O'Keefe, Minister of State at the Department of Foreign Affairs, said of the Community's role: 'If the EEC has a fault, it is that it doesn't demand an equal response from other developed countries.'

IRELAND'S ROLE

Ireland's main links with the Third World have traditionally been through the missionary orders. In the mid 1970s there were 4,600 Irish missionary personnel working in developing countries making a major contribution through their schools and hospitals. Ireland has sent people rather than money to the Third World. While the missionaries have received generous support from the public and while voluntary organisations were active in promoting Third World development, Irish governments were slow to adopt an official aid policy for the Third World. Prior to 1973 official development aid came in response to requests for assistance from international organisations such as the United Nations.

1973 has been described as a watershed in the evolution of an Irish policy on official development aid. Accession to the EEC stimulated official thinking about the Third World. The Community was committed to playing an enlightened role in relations with developing countries and as a member of the Community, Ireland had to accept a new responsibility. Garret FitzGerald became Minister for Foreign Affairs in the same year, bringing to the office a long-standing interest in development policy. In 1974 he established an Agency for Personal Services Overseas (APSO), which provides 75% of the cost of services by Irish people working in the Third World in hospitals and universities and for organisations such as Gorta, Concern and Irish state-sponsored bodies. APSO has helped fund about 1,100 overseas assignments for Irish people. The minister also initiated a bi-lateral aid policy, to run parallel with increased commitments to EEC multi-lateral aid programmes, whereby Ireland would fund projects directly in selected developing countries. A new section of the Department of Foreign Affairs was set up to administer the policy. The countries chosen for aid were India, Lesotho, Sudan, Tanzania and Zambia. Even more significantly, the minister announced that the government intended to increase the resources allocated in official development aid year by year until it reached the target of 0.7% of gross national product recommended by the United Nations and endorsed by the EEC.

These new commitments in turn encouraged other initiatives. State-sponsored bodies with an interest in providing development expertise to developing countries agreed to establish a coordinating agency known as DEVCO. The universities and third-level colleges established an organisation known as HEDCO, to provide educational expertise to the Third World.

Official development aid has increased considerably, if unevenly, since the early 1970s. Official development assistance for 1983 was IR£30 million, just over one-third of which was for bi-lateral aid. The remainder represents our commitments to Community or UN multilateral development policies. At 0.23% of GNP this represents a considerable increase on 0.05% in 1972 but is far short of the level of 0.7% of GNP which is still the official target. Our performance lags behind most of our partners in the Community, some of whom have exceeded the UN recommended level of GNP in official development aid. Looked at from another angle, Ireland is actually making a profit from development assistance. DEVCO estimated that in 1980 Irish state-sponsored bodies earned 40% more from the supply of services to the Third World than it gave in the entire official development assistance programme for the same year. On trade with newly industrialising countries Ireland has taken a protectionist stance, supporting a restrictive EEC line during renegotiation of the multi-fibre textile arrangement.

Non-governmental agencies working in the Third World such as Trocaire, Concern and Gorta, have benefited from the growth of development policy at national and Community level although the bulk of their funds came direct from public appeals. Government and Community funding is available to voluntary organisations working in Third World countries for development projects under the bi-lateral aid programme and under the second Lomé convention from the European development fund. Funding these projects gives these organisations a measure of involvement in official aid programmes and, at the same time, provides assistance for small-scale, community-based projects. In 1980, the Minister' for Foreign Affairs, Brian Lenihan, established an Advisory Council on Development Cooperation, broadly representative of all sectors of society and including experts from the aid organisations, to assist in the formulation and review of policy towards the Third World.

The main reason given for the slow growth in the proportion of aid to the Third World is the economic difficulties which the country has faced since the oil crisis of 1973. These difficulties pale into insignificance, however, when compared to the difficulties of Third World countries. Ireland is the twenty-fourth richest country in the world out of a total of 150, with a per capita GNP thirty-six times greater than that of the poorest nations. The recession has hit the poorest countries in the Third World more severely than the poorer industrialised countries. Even on economic grounds a generous aid and trade programme for the Third World makes sense. While our trade with the Third World is small in volume terms, it is increasing faster than trade with industrialised countries. If Third World economies are crippled by payments for oil, food and interest charges on debts they will not have sufficient money to buy Irish-manufactured goods. Limiting the access of Third World goods to Irish markets may save marginal jobs in the short term but by reducing the earnings of developing countries it will prevent them from buying products which Ireland can produce competitively. As a small open economy dependent on access to the markets of the world, Ireland has a vested interest in promoting free trade and equity in the international economy.

EMS — the 1978 Bore of the Year Award.

Donal Foley in 'Man Bites Dog'

132

16
The European Monetary System

COMMISSIONER DICK BURKE was in relaxed form with a group of journalists at a lunch in Brussels in December 1978 when one of his cabinet advisers, Liam Hourican, was called to the phone. On his return Liam announced that the Taoiseach, Jack Lynch, had decided that Ireland would join the European monetary system (EMS). 'The same again, waiter,' said Mr Burke. 'This is a great day for Ireland.' Within an hour Mr Burke had issued a statement saying: 'The establishment of the European monetary system is an historic event for the Community, and Ireland's full involvement from the outset must be a cause of satisfaction.'

The EMS was indeed a new phase in Europe's efforts to achieve monetary stability. The customs union and the common agricultural policy were set up during the period of stable exchange rates, when it was assumed that the unity of the market would lead to economic convergence. Economic and monetary union was not defined by the Treaty of Rome, but in 1962 the Commission called for coordination of the monetary policies of the

Six, and in 1964 committees of central bank governors and budget experts were constituted, the former to improve monetary policy, the latter to compare national budget policies. By the end of the 1960s anxiety at the growing currency instability had inspired studies on an economic and monetary union (the Barre and Werner Reports).

Economic and monetary union by 1980 was the goal proclaimed by the Six in The Hague in 1969 and this was endorsed by the Nine in Paris in 1972, but the details were left vague. An attempt by the member states to align their currencies against the dollar in a system known as 'the snake' achieved only limited success.

European monetary union implies that governments surrender their control of exchange rates and monetary policies to an EEC Central Bank and that a central budgetary authority control fiscal and budgetary policy, determine income and regional policies and define medium-term policies.

Such a concept became as unreal as Disneyland during the 1974-75 recession when the member states reacted disjointedly to the impact of the oil-price rises. The only common response was to jealously guard their national control of monetary policy instruments. In vain, the Commission sought powers to determine the economic policies of the members. Instead of advances being made towards monetary union there was movement backwards by the late 1970s. Never in twenty-five years had the national monetary and economic policies been more divergent. So fashionable was it to mock monetary union that it came as a surprise in October 1977 when Commission President Roy Jenkins rehabilitated the cause in a Jean Monnet lecture that was noted with interest in Paris and Bonn.

The main factor in reviving efforts to establish monetary stability in Europe was the steep fall in the dollar during the presidency of Jimmy Carter. President Giscard d'Estaing and Chancellor Schmidt agreed that the Community should take a fresh initiative to shield Community currencies from the adverse effects of the dollar's slide. It was the Paris-Bonn alliance that dominated the shape of the European monetary system, which came into operation in March 1979, as the first step towards the creation of 'a zone of monetary stability in Europe'.

Britain's refusal to join the new system presented Ireland with a difficult choice of breaking the link with sterling and taking the risks of an independent currency, or of sticking with the pound and remaining aloof from an important step in Community integration. The difficulty which a break with sterling would cause in relations with Northern Ireland was another factor to be considered. The decision whether or not to join was made even more difficult for Taoiseach Jack Lynch when, near the end of negotiations, France opposed extra transfers to Ireland from the regional fund to compensate for the economic sacrifices required under the new system. This setback was compounded for Mr Lynch when journalists reported him as saying that Ireland had been offered a package of loans and interest-rate subsidies of £225 million over five years when instead he had said that it amounted to £1125 million in loans over five years, £225 million of which would be given as an interest-rate lump sum.

Either figure fell far short of the £650 million direct grant aid requested by the government earlier in the negotiations for investment in infrastructure and industrial development. At the last minute Ireland was offered a further special loan of £50 million for two years. This was sufficient to swing the balance in favour of Ireland's membership of the new system.

The EMS is an exchange-rate system in which the members align the value of their currencies in a stable but adjustable relationship. A European currency unit - the ECU - which is a basket average of the participating currencies, is at the centre of the system. ECUs are supplied to the central banks by the European monetary cooperation fund against the deposit of 20% of their gold and 20% of their dollar reserves. These swap arrangements are renewed every three months.

Each currency has a central rate against the ECU. A parity grid system of cross rates established the value of each currency against the others. Around market exchange rates fluctuation margins of 2.25% are allowed - for Italy it is 6% - above and below them. Like a see-saw, if a currency hits the bottom margin against another the central banks of the two countries intervene to buy the weaker and sell the stronger currencies, thus restoring stability.

An ECU basket formula is also used as an indicator to detect a 'deviant' currency. If a currency diverges from the other currencies and crosses a 'threshold of divergence' - fixed at 75% of the maximum spread of divergences for each currency - it is presumed that corrective action will be taken by the national authorities.

Safety nets are also provided to assist currencies that are in difficulty. There is unlimited immediate financing for forty-five days, with a possible extension of three months, to protect the parity grid; a short-term credit of fourteen billion ECU to support a currency whose reserves are threatened; and medium term financial assistance (fourteen billion ECU) provides credit for two to five years for those countries suffering severe balance-of-payments problems.

At their European Council in Bremen in July 1978 the heads of government announced that within two years of the setting up of the EMS they would establish a European monetary fund and would transform the ECU, an accountancy unit, into a reserve asset and a means of settlement between banks. Provision was made for adjustments - a euphemism for changing the value of currencies - to be done with the agreement of all

the members. There were seven changes in EMS central rates between
March 1979 and March 1983.

Table 7

Changes in EMS Central Rates

(revaluation +, devaluation −)

1979		%
24 Sept.	German mark	+2
	Danish krone	−2.9
30 Nov.	Danish krone	+4.8
1981		
20 March	Italian lira	−6
04 Oct.	French franc	−3
	Italian lira	−3
	German mark	+5.5
	Dutch guilder	+5.5
1982		
21 Feb.	Belgian franc	−8.5
	Danish krone	−3
13 June	French franc	−5.75
	Italian lira	−2.75
	German mark	+4.25
	Dutch guilder	+4.25
1983		
21 March	French franc	−4.5
	Italian lira	−2.5
	Irish pound	−3.5
	German mark	+5.5
	Dutch guilder	+3.5
	Danish krone	+2.5
	Belgian franc	+1.5

For political reasons the French and German leaders blocked the move
to the next stage of establishing a European monetary fund. Central banks,
not least the powerful German Bundesbank, did not want to relinquish
prerogatives to a new European fund. As a result, EEC finance ministers
have ignored Commission proposals advocating greater use of the ECU,
and other developments of the system.

A report by the European Parliament's Committee on Economic and Monetary Affairs in February 1984 noted that the second oil crisis of 1979 disrupted the recovery that had been taking place from the first oil embargo of 1973/74. 'Both the widely varying dependence of member states on oil imports and the diversity of the policies adopted to combat balance-of-payments difficulties encouraged the divergence of economic trends and increased inflation-rate differentials,' it said.

Despite these difficulties the EMS has given relative stability to the EMS currencies and has decreased their volatility against the dollar, the yen and sterling. Countries like France, Italy and Ireland, where inflation was highest, sustained less of a decline in effective exchange rates than had been the case pre-EMS. And according to the Parliament's report, this relative stability resulted from central bank intervention and the economic discipline of some member states. But the central banks, especially the Bundesbank, intervened in either dollars or in Community currencies rather than in ECUs. There had been virtually no recourse to short-term monetary support or medium-term financial assistance except for France in 1983.

A number of weaknesses were highlighted by the report:
- The three-month ECU swap system creates ECUs blindly at a rate determined not by member states' borrowing needs but by variations in the price of gold and the rate of the dollar. This arbitrary and potentially inflationary creation of ECUs does not allow the ECU to ease difficulties arising from the fluctuation of the dollar.
- The German mark is vulnerable to money movements from or to the dollar. This causes the mark to fluctuate for reasons unconnected with the economic variables affecting relations between the Community countries. Furthermore, the interventions by the central banks in dollars, regardless of US balance-of-payments trends, runs contrary to the aim of shielding the EMS from dollar fluctuations.
- The ECU is not widely accepted in bank settlements. If a debt, denominated in ECUs, is not repaid early, the creditor bank is obliged to accept no more than 50% of the repayment in ECUs.
- There has been little convergence of prices and costs in the economies of member states.

The Parliament has therefore backed the Commission in urging EEC governments to consolidate the EMS and has appealed to Britain to join the exchange-rate system. The ECU should be allowed to cooperate more with the dollar and the yen in furthering international exchange-rate stability.

The main reason Ireland joined this exchange-rate system was because it aspired to the low inflation and interest-rate levels enjoyed by West

Germany. There were instances of government ministers telling the unions that they would have to adjust to West German style discipline on the wages front. If the Irish government thought that the punt would be a stronger currency than sterling, they were soon disappointed. Soon after the break, sterling soared in value above the Irish punt on the strength of North Sea oil and a new Conservative government.

In swapping John Bull for the Euro-corset the government also made other miscalculations. Instead of dropping, inflation rose from 11.5% to over 20%; interest rates rose to unprecedented levels and for most of the time the punt was worth only 78 pence sterling. High rates of domestic inflation reduced the competitiveness of Irish exports. If it were not for the rise in the value of sterling after 1979, manufacturing firms exporting to the British market would have been more severely hit. Firms exporting to the stronger EMS countries suffered badly. Agriculture, in which about 40% of exports are to Britain, was unable to devalue the green pound to the income benefit of farmers because the scope for currency adjustments had been removed by the EMS. Domestically, governments pursued a programme of high public expenditure which meant a policy of foreign borrowing. Most of the country's economic transactions continue to be in dollars or sterling rather than in EMS currencies.

Joining the EMS also increased the importance of the border as an economic barrier between the two parts of the island. Before 1979 sterling circulated freely in the Republic but since then Northerners have had to change their pounds into punts before coming south. It complicates business transactions for firms operating on both sides of the border and is another division adding to those already existing on the island. Joining the EMS in 1979 may have been the right thing to do but it might have made better economic sense to retain the link with sterling and to have sought a lower exchange rate for the Irish pound.

17
Regional Policy

The human face of the Community.

APART FROM THE prospect of a price bonanza for farmers, a main attraction for Ireland of EEC membership was the promise of a regional fund that would bring living standards closer to those enjoyed in the more prosperous parts of the Community. A major concern of Irish governments in the accession negotiations was preventing or at least minimising job losses in the manufacturing sector as a result of the removal of protection and the likely pull of investment to the more developed regions on the continent. Accordingly, a protocol was included in the Accession Treaty in which the Community took note of the fact 'that the Irish government has embarked upon the implementation of a policy of industrialisation and economic development designed to align the standard of living in Ireland with those of the other European nations and to eliminate under-employment while progressively evening out regional differences in levels of development.' The other member states recognised that competition rules needed to be applied in a way that took account of the objectives of the government's economic expansion programme to raise living standards.

As a result the government was allowed retain, for a temporary period, export sales relief - the special tax concession on profits from exports, the main incentive to foreign firms to come to this country. Following prolonged negotiations, the Commission agreed in 1980 to allow firms which already enjoyed export-sales relief to retain the concession but other firms were to substitute a low rate of corporation tax - 10% - on their profits. This tax conforms more to the rules of the Community because it does not discriminate between firms producing for the home market and for export, while recognising Ireland's need to provide greater incentives for industrial investment than more developed regions of the Community.

As Taoiseach, Jack Lynch took part in the 1972 Paris summit at which the European leaders agreed that 'a high priority should be given to the aim of correcting, in the Community, the structural and regional imbalances which might affect the realisation of economic and monetary union.' Agreeing to coordinate their regional policies and to attempt to find a Community solution to regional problems, the leaders invited the EEC Commission, the Council of Ministers and the Parliament to cooperate in setting up a regional development fund by the end of 1973.

Along with moves towards economic and monetary union, it was agreed that efforts would have to be made to assist Ireland, which was the poorest member state; Greenland, which was dependent on Denmark; the industrially declining regions of the United Kingdom, including Scotland, Northern Ireland and the north of England; and deprived regions - such as Italy's Mezzogiorno - which had failed to enjoy the prosperity achieved by the richer member states of the Community in the 1960s. Though the EEC averaged a 5.4% growth rate throughout the 1960s the gap between the richest and poorest regions measured as a proportion of gross domestic product remained at 5 to 1. The problem, however, was that the Treaty of Rome did not provide for a regional policy though the Treaty advocates 'continued and balanced expansion in member states'. Accordingly, the member states fell back on an 'umbrella' clause provided in Article 235 of the Treaty under which they justified the instruction to set up such a policy. Article 235 states: 'If action by the Community should prove necessary to attain, in the course of the operation of the common market, one of the objectives of the Community and this Treaty has not provided the necessary powers, the Council shall, acting unanimously on a proposal from the Commission and after consulting the Assembly, take the appropriate measures.'

In 1973 the Commission put forward proposals for a European regional development fund (ERDF) and a Regional Policy Committee which would complement the efforts of national governments to assist underdeveloped regions. It suggested that aid be concentrated on those regions where the gross domestic product was consistently below the national average, in which there was an over-dependence on agriculture or a declining industry and with consistently high rates of unemployment. The blueprint favoured a fund of £1,000 million with the ERDF operating in much the same way as the social fund.

Few things illustrate more clearly the different climate of Community decision-making in the 1970s compared to the late 1950s than the way in which the Commission's proposals for a regional policy were handled by the member states. At the December 1974 Paris summit the European leaders rejected most of the Commission's plan and substituted a meagre alternative. They could only agree to a fund of £542 million for the three-year period 1975-77. Instead of concentration on the most deprived regions, the areas eligible for assistance covered 55% of the surface area of the Community, containing 35% of its population. Aid was to be distributed according to strict national quotas on the following basis:

Belgium	1.5%	Luxembourg	0.1%
Denmark	1.3%	Netherlands	1.7%
France	15%	West Germany	6.4%
Ireland	6%	United Kingdom	28%
Italy	40%		

Irish Foreign Minister Garret FitzGerald had fought for a bigger fund and a further ½% was allocated to Ireland, to be deducted from the share of the others except for Italy. On this basis Ireland was allocated £35 million.

Commenting on the summit decision *The Irish Times* noted that 'Dr FitzGerald can claim some satisfaction from the creation of any fund at all, but this one is painfully small and must represent both a disappointment and a setback in the continuing negotiation which is membership of the Community. A larger fund would have been a firmer assurance that the goal of balanced development is being taken seriously.' The coalition government described the £35 million as 'small but significant' but the opposition party, Fianna Fáil, dismissed it as 'ludicrous and insulting'.

As part of the package it was agreed that all of Ireland, North and South, should qualify for regional aid. Northern Ireland was clearly the most deprived region of the United Kingdom but the classification of the whole of the Republic as an underdeveloped region was not so obvious. In the event our partners accepted the government argument that unless the whole country benefited from regional aid, it would be unable to take on Community tasks arising from economic and monetary union. This concession probably increased Ireland's overall share of the fund to 6%, 2% more than the country could claim on the basis of its share of Community population but it ignored the disparities between different parts of Ireland, disparities which were explicitly recognised in the protocol to the Treaty of Accession. Recent figures from the Central Statistics Office show that while average weekly household income in the east of Ireland is IR£137, in Donegal and the north west it is only IR£68, a difference as great as many to be found between Ireland and richer regions of the Community.

The ERDF, which began operations in 1975, lends money for three main kinds of projects:
- Industrial, handicraft and service industries, including tourism, which are economically sound and which benefit from state or local authority aids and which provide a minimum of ten jobs or maintain ten existing jobs.
- Infrastructure projects wholly or partly financed by a public authority and which contribute to the development of a region. A maximum of 70% of fund money was earmarked for this purpose but this figure has been exceeded.
- Infrastructure in mountain and hill farming areas and for farming in less favoured areas.

In a review of the ERDF in 1978, it was agreed to keep 5% of the money available outside the system of national quotas. The Commission and the Regional Policy Committee were not given the power to decide how this money should be spent. National control was maintained by the proviso that the Council of Ministers had to give unanimous approval to any project financed from non-quota moneys.

In Ireland, water and sewerage projects have received the largest amount of support from the ERDF to date, about one-third of the total. Telecommunications, roads and industrial estates figure high on the list of assisted projects, reflecting the backwardness of Irish industrial infrastructure.

A symbolic package of aids for cross-border development was approved by the Council of Ministers in 1980, as a result of cooperation between Dublin and Belfast, providing IR£10.7 million to the Republic of Ireland and £4.4 million sterling to Northern Ireland up to 1985. The aid helps the development of tourism, communications, and the management of small and medium-sized enterprises.

On the accession of Greece to the Community, Ireland's share of the ERDF was reduced slightly to 5.94%. In the second phase of the fund, 1978-80, Ireland was allocated £75 million of a total fund of £1200 million, a total which Regional Commissioner Antonio Giolitti complained was too small to make a dent in the regional problems. Although Ireland had earlier championed the Commission's proposal for a bigger fund, Mr Lynch, accompanied by Foreign Minister Michael O'Kennedy, professed to be pleased with the renewal of the fund at the Brussels European Council in December 1977.

Originally, it was intended that EEC regional aid should supplement the already devised programmes of governments for regional expansion. But in practice ERDF allocations find their way into national exchequers so that it is virtually impossible to say whether these grants are additional or not to national regional expenditure. It is not clear either whether the ERDF has stimulated increased regional spending by governments. In Ireland's case receipts are listed in the annual public capital programme by the Department of Finance, which can be used, according to departmental discretion, for what is deemed most advantageous - be it an advance factory in Mayo or the Matt Talbot bridge in Dublin.

Because Ireland was designated as one region under the ERDF, the Department of Finance obtained a monopoly control of the disbursement of funds in this country. The extent of its discretionary powers over this disbursement was highlighted during the controversy over the cost of the rapid rail system in Dublin. CIE's new electrified rail system was approved for assistance from the ERDF but, late in the day, the Department of Finance withheld the money and informed the company that it would have to borrow the money instead.

One paradox of the immature Community regional policy is that it has effectively scotched domestic concern for formulating a balanced development of all the regions in the country. Only 40% of ERDF aid to Ireland has gone to projects in the least developed counties. It is no coincidence that Irish governments have been silent on internal regional policy since the pre-membership date of 1972. A report from the National Economic and Social Council in 1978 pointed out that there was no clearly articulated policy for regional economic development. The government showed its insensitivity to regional issues by submitting the White Paper on National Development 1977-80, as its central document in the Community's regional development programme for Ireland, 1977-80. On Ireland's designation as one region, John Healy has commented that this 'politically neat device . . . militates against the obviously poorer regions of the country when it comes to funding projects from the regional development fund.'

The EEC regional policy has many weaknesses. The ERDF is too small to reduce regional disparities and the national quotas limit the extent to which disparities between the richest and poorest regions can be narrowed. Ireland's position, relative to the average gross domestic product per head in the Community, has worsened slightly since joining the EEC, mainly because of the rapid increase in population. The absence of Community-based criteria for the application of aid and the requirement that it be paid direct to the government of the receiving country limits the discretion of the Commission, by comparison with the more '*communautaire*' social fund. The Commission and the European Parliament would like to see a greatly increased ERDF. The richer member states have been unwilling to increase their contributions to the ERDF and have been more impressed by arguments for increases in farm spending than by the need to reduce regional disparities.

Ireland would like to see a larger ERDF, but not if it means less support for dairy farming or beef, as this is of far greater financial benefit to the country than even the most generous fund proposed. A further drawback of the present system is that when the Community is enlarged to include Spain and Portugal, Ireland's existing small share of the fund will fall further because of the problems of underdevelopment in the two applicant countries. The Court of Auditors has declared that the ERDF would be more effective in correcting regional imbalances if it concentrated on priority areas and the Court has expressed disappointment that the regional programmes submitted by governments were so vague.

NEW PROPOSALS

Since 1981 the Commission has argued for a more radical regional policy. It favours replacing rigid quotas with a flexible range of assistance criteria within which regions could benefit. The range proposed for Ireland is 5.05% to 7.13% of a larger fund. The Commission would like to reduce the extent to which governments substitute ERDF funds for national expenditure and the amount of assistance to once-off projects. It proposed that 40% of the ERDF should be allocated by the Commission to operations which form part of an overall development plan for each region. The remainder of the money would be available to assist national programmes of Community interest, initiated by member states as at present.

One implication of the new programme is that the Commission would have direct contact with regional development authorities, contact which governments have resisted up to now. This is particularly true of successive Irish governments which have used the Community's designation of the country as one region as a justification for maintaining tight control of ERDF applications. There is, however, a growing demand from underdeveloped regions throughout the Community for a greater say in decisions made about them. This has arisen partly from the realisation that one of the reasons for the backwardness of some regions is their distance from the centres of power and the absence of effective decision-making power at regional level. A political infrastructure may be as important as a physical infrastructure in the development of backward economies.

The Parliament, whose members are elected on a regional basis, has taken a particular interest in the operation of the regional policy and has campaigned for a larger ERDF and more discretion to the Commission. In early 1984 it sponsored a conference in Strasbourg on the regions and this conference emphasised the need for devolution of decision-making. It also highlighted the ambiguity at the heart of the regional policy as it affects Ireland. If it is desirable that Ireland should benefit from transfers from the wealthy parts of the Community, it is equally desirable that the poorer parts of the country should benefit from an indigenous regional policy.

EUROPEAN INVESTMENT BANK

The European Investment Bank (EIB), from modest beginnings, has become a major instrument of Community regional policy. The Bank, removed from the direct control of the Council of Ministers, has a low profile and its activities are not well known. Set up by the Treaty, it has a legal, financial and administrative identity separate from the other institutions of the Community and is given the task of helping the Community's smooth and balanced development. The Bank, a non-profit organisation, raises money on the world capital market on the strength of contributions made by each member state to the Bank's capital. In 1982 Noel Whelan became the first Irish person to be appointed Vice-President of the Bank.

The EIB lends money for projects which assist regional development, promote an interest common to several member states, and modernise or convert enterprises in sectors faced with particular problems. All assisted projects must contribute to increased economic productivity. The main activity of the Bank is assisting regional development; about 70% of lending to date has been for this purpose. The Bank is not obliged to lend according to quotas but judges projects on their economic merits.

The EIB's role has been greatly extended by the introduction of what is known as the 'new Community instrument' (or the 'Ortoli facility' named after the Commissioner who sponsored it). Under this arrangement, the Commission raises money in capital markets for investment, while the Bank administers the loans. These loans are used to support projects in key fields mainly for investment in infrastructure and industry and for conservation of energy.

The Bank's contribution to Irish development has been enhanced by the establishment of the European monetary system in 1979. As part of the agreement on the EMS it was agreed that for the period 1978-83 the two poorest members of the new system, Ireland and Italy, would be entitled to grants equivalent to 3% interest on loans from the EIB. Between 1973 and 1983 the Bank has lent Ireland IR£1441.5 million, or about 10% of its total Bank lending. The money has provided, amongst other things, 700 advance factories, helped to plant 100,000 acres of new forest, given assistance to 1,200 small and medium-sized industries and services, and contributed to the electrification of the Dublin suburban railway, the construction of the natural gas pipeline from Cork to Dublin and the ESB power station at Moneypoint, Co. Clare. The failure of the regional fund to develop has increased the role and importance of the Bank as a source of finance for underdeveloped regions.

A former Irish Minister for Agriculture was a total abstainer. At a ministerial party in Brussels his French host offered him one drink after another which the Irishman firmly refused, pointing to his pioneer pin. The French minister notices the pin but did not understand its significance. Puzzled, it was not until late in the evening that he suddenly understood why the Irishman was not drinking. Apologising profusely he said: 'I'm so sorry, I didn't realise that you had a heart condition'.

18
Social Affairs

'What will the EEC do for us?'

THE EEC FOUNDERS were torn between a desire for a free market and apprehension about its consequences. Economic progress for the population as a whole could mean reduced living standards for a minority. The social provisions in the Treaty were intended to promote competition while protecting vulnerable groups and regions from the adverse effects of unrestricted competition. The Treaty obliged the Community to allow free movement of workers and employed persons, ensuring that national laws would not prevent mobility of labour. It outlawed different rates of pay for men and women for work of equal value because such differentials would distort the costs of production. More positively, the Community was given power to improve living and working conditions, to harmonise conditions of employment, labour law, training, social security, to prevent occupational accidents and disease and ensure the right of association and collective bargaining. A social fund was to be set up to finance these

147

activities. The common thread running through this range of activities is that they are all related to the operation of the common market and the conditions governing the employment of workers. The Treaty did not give the Community competence to develop a comprehensive policy to cover the broad spectrum of social problems in the Community. Despite this handicap, the Community has an impressive track record on social issues where it has power to act.

MOVEMENT OF WORKERS AND SOCIAL SECURITY

The Community moved quickly to remove restrictions on the movement of workers from one member state to another. The loss of entitlement to social security benefits when a worker moved to another member state was a major deterrent to mobility. Community rules now guarantee equal social security treatment for workers of Community origin and their families, giving them the right to exactly the same social security protection as nationals of the host country. A worker may claim benefits for his or her family, even if they are living in another member state. For pension purposes, workers can add together their periods of social insurance in various member countries and claim social security pension in whichever member state they choose to settle. This affects many Irish people who, having spent their working lives in Britain or Northern Ireland, are entitled to a UK pension if they decide to retire to the Republic.

Migrant workers are also entitled to social assistance services on the same basis as nationals of the member states. This means that EEC nationals in this country are entitled to children's allowances, unmarried mother's allowance, unemployment and other allowances on the same basis as Irish nationals. Irish citizens in other member states may claim equivalent benefits. In 1982 these arrangements were extended to self-employed workers moving to other member states, although family allowances were excluded from the range of benefits they could claim. Unlike other member states, self-employed workers in Ireland are not insured, as a result of which the range of services available to self-employed workers coming from other member states in Ireland is small. If Irish nationals are not entitled to the service, EEC nationals in the same categories do not have entitlement.

Citizens of one member state are entitled to medical care when they go to another member state under exactly the same financial terms as citizens of the host state. The Irish government has interpreted its obligations liberally in this regard and has gone beyond the minimum required by Community legislation. All EEC nationals, regardless of income, are entitled to the same range of services as Irish people with full eligibility - free drugs, free general practitioner, hospital and consultant services and a range of other preventive services. Under Community arrangements a

148

member state may reimburse another for treating its nationals or the families of migrant workers who remain in their country of origin, but, in view of the small numbers involved, Ireland has non-reimbursement arrangements with eight of the member states. Because of the number of Irish people working in the UK with families in Ireland and the number of UK pensioners resident in Ireland, a reimbursement arrangement based on a lump sum payment has been agreed. In 1983 the refund from the UK government amounted to a substantial IR£25 million.

Irish citizens visiting another member state on business or for holidays have the right to health care under exactly the same financial terms as citizens of the host state. Most health services in member states are free at the point of delivery but in some, charges are made for certain services. In Belgium patients are normally required to pay 20% of the cost of general practitioner treatment, while in France hospital patients may be charged, with subsequent reimbursement for those in need. To claim the right to medical services in all member states except the UK the person travelling must apply beforehand to their health board for a special form known as an EIII to establish his or her entitlement. No forms are required for those visiting the UK. Detailed information on social security and medical entitlements in other member states is available from health board offices, the Department of Health or the Office of the European Communities in Dublin.

THE SOCIAL ACTION PROGRAMME

Apart from the movement of workers and the harmonisation of social security the social aspects of integration received little attention in the 1960s. The activities of the social fund were mostly confined to retraining workers in obsolete industries. As the decade wore on there was disenchantment in member states with post-war economic policies and institutions. The Community was increasingly criticised for its preoccupation with economics and accused of being a rich man's club. The European leaders, especially Georges Pompidou, Edward Heath and Willy Brandt, responded to the challenge by deciding that the Community should be given a human face. At the Paris summit of 1972 the heads of government announced that, for them, vigorous social action was as important as economic and monetary union. This gave the Commission the opening it needed to put forward ideas on how the social provisions of the Treaty could be met.

In January 1974 Dr Hillery's Social Affairs Directorate in the Commission won agreement from the Council for a social action programme which forms the Community's agenda on social affairs to the present day. The action programme outlined three main objectives:

Full and Better Employment   When the action programme was drawn up there was little evidence that Europe was on the eve of the most severe recession of this century. Unemployment throughout the Community averaged 2%. The Commission was primarily concerned with both regional unemployment and structural unemployment as technical advance accelerated. The emphasis was on retraining workers, guaranteeing them an income during training and providing information on job opportunities in other parts of the Community. In addition the Commission was concerned about the special problems faced by particular groups of workers on the labour market - migrant workers from outside the Community, women, elderly workers, the handicapped and school leavers.

Improvement of Living and Working Conditions   In setting out its proposals the Commission was motivated by the comparative poverty in which many people lived and by the disparity between rich and poor countries. Inadequate housing, the length of working hours, inequalities between men's and women's pay and the boredom of many jobs were also on its list of problems to be tackled. The programme proposed studies to assess the extent and nature of poverty in the Community and an institute to study how working conditions could be improved.

Greater Participation   The Commission proposed increased participation by the social partners in Community decision-making and by workers in the affairs of their companies.

IMPLEMENTATION

While the recession undermined many of the assumptions of the programme, considerable progress was made in implementing its proposals. The role of the social fund was substantially widened in 1973 and 1978 to enable it to support vocational training for a much wider range of people, to finance work-experience programmes and schemes to combat poverty and to give additional assistance to particularly deprived regions such as Ireland and Northern Ireland. The European Foundation for the Improvement of Living and Working Conditions was established in Dublin in 1977. The Foundation undertakes research and advises the Community on the policies it should pursue on issues such as shift-work, new forms of work organisation and improvements in safety and health at work. In the same year the European Centre for the Development of Vocational Training was set up in Berlin.

A directive on collective redundancies in 1975 led to major changes in Irish legislation governing redundancies. A further directive, agreed in July 1982, protects workers from exposure to lead and its by-products, a measure which must be complied with in all member states by January 1986. In

1975 the Council recommended that the principle of the forty-hour week and four weeks paid annual holiday for each worker be implemented in member states and in 1982 they recommended that flexible retirement ages for work be progressively introduced. A draft directive on the protection of the rights of part-time workers is before the Council which would give such workers proportional rights with regard to pay, holidays, redundancy and pensions. A directive obliging large companies to disclose information about the activities of their companies is also at an advanced stage. (For the impact of Community directives on the conditions of employment of women see Chapter 19).

The Community's programme to combat poverty, initiated in 1975, was of particular interest to Ireland. The Commission proposed the establishment of a number of pilot projects to assess the extent and nature of poverty in the Community. The poor were defined as those individuals and families whose resources were so small as to exclude them from the minimum acceptable way of life of the country in which they lived. Anyone who did not earn half the average income of the country in which they lived was defined as poor. The Commission's proposals were supported enthusiastically by the Irish government in the person of Frank Cluskey and twenty-four pilot projects were put forward for Community assistance, by far the largest number in any member state. (Two projects were agreed for Northern Ireland.) The work of the pilot schemes in the Republic was coordinated by a national committee chaired by Sr Stanislaus Kennedy. Although the committee and some of the schemes were dogged by dissension and controversy, the general consensus is that they did worthwhile work in collecting information about poverty, in helping the poor acquire their rights and in raising living standards through vocational training, improved housing and health care. When the pilot projects came to an end in 1980 the results of the national projects were assembled in a Community report which left no room for complacency about poverty. Poverty in member states was found to be increasing because of the recession and to be primarily associated with unemployment. Poverty among the unemployed was most serious where there were large numbers of dependent children or when the adult was a single parent. In marginal social groups such as gypsies, travellers and migrant workers the social handicaps of one generation are passed on to the next. The report pointed to the need for concerted action by member states at Community and national level to abolish poverty but so far there is little evidence of the necessary commitment.

THE EUROPEAN SOCIAL FUND

The activities of the social fund are so important that they are often equated unfairly with the entire social programme of the Community. The social fund is the financial instrument through which the Community achieves its social objectives in the labour market. It improves employment opportunities by giving aid to schemes which without fund assistance would not come into existence. Every five years the rules of the fund are reviewed in order to make its activities relevant to the changes in the labour market. The latest review took place in 1983 when a new emphasis was given to training unemployed young people who now constitute five million of the twelve million unemployed in the Community. A total of 75% of fund spending must go to schemes to help people under twenty-five years of age. The aim is to give young people leaving education a 'social guarantee' of a choice of work experience or vocational training; because of the numbers of young people relative to the size of its population, Ireland is likely to benefit considerably from the new arrangements. In addition, the fund will continue to help the handicapped, workers from redundant industries, women and deprived groups, with the proviso that 40% of all social fund spending must go to the priority regions of the Community - Ireland, Northern Ireland, Greece, southern Italy and the overseas departments.

The overall aim of the new rules is to make the fund a real weapon in the fight against unemployment, as distinct from its original task in promoting vocational training, a change which Michael O'Leary as Minister for Labour fought for in the 1970s. Its success in achieving this aim will depend on the amount of money which the finance ministers commit to the fund. While the social affairs ministers have competence to decide on the categories of aid to be provided by the fund, it is the finance ministers who decide on the amount of money available - the finance ministers annoyed their colleagues during the 1970s by limiting the amount of money available for young people.

Unlike the regional fund, money from the social fund does not have to be allocated according to national quotas. Decisions on applications for assistance are taken by an advisory committee of officials from the Commission and the member states, with representatives from employer and trade union groups. Decisions are based on the rules laid down by the Council on the number and quality of the applications and the priorities of the Committee. There are usually many more applications than funds. Applications from the public sector in member states stand a better chance of acceptance than those from the private sector. The fund can meet 50% of the costs of a project, although in the priority regions the ceiling is 55%. Once aid has been agreed, 30% is paid in advance, a further 30% at the half-way stage and the remainder on completion. Benefiting organisations receive assistance direct from the fund.

Former Secretary of the Department of Labour, Tadhg O Cearbhaill, has noted that 'the results of the social fund can be seen more clearly in Ireland than in any other member state' (*Community Report*, January 1983). The principal operations receiving social fund assistance in this country up to 1983 were:
- training and retraining of unemployed workers
- training of workers for new industries
- upgrading skills of existing workers
- training of apprentices, technicians and middle managers
- training of the disabled and handicapped
- job creation programmes, i.e. the work experience programme and the employment incentive schemes.

The main organisations assisted by the fund were The Industrial Training Authority (AnCO), the Industrial Development Authority (IDA), Shannon Free Airport Development Company (SFADCo), Udaras na Gaeltachta, Bord Iascaigh Mhara (BIM), CERT (Hotel Staff Training Body), The Electricity Supply Board (ESB), The Irish Management Institute (IMI), The Youth Employment Agency (YEA), the National Rehabilitation Board (NRB) and the Departments of Labour, Education and the Environment. Thanks to social fund assistance, AnCO training places rose from 1,000 in 1973 to 5,550 in 1981. The number of workers trained for new industries rose from 2,300 to 9,500 in the same period. The rise in the number of places for the handicapped was even larger. Between 1973 and the end of 1982, IR£345 million was paid by the fund to assist projects in this country, money which would otherwise not have been available to assist vocational training or job creation. While major problems remain in the Irish labour market, there is no doubt about the important contribution which the Community has made to assisting national programmes to train workers for new kinds of industry nor that unemployment would be a great deal worse without that assistance.

19
Women and the EEC

Louise Weiss welcomes Simone Veil as the first President of the directly elected Parliament in 1979.

THE FOUNDING 'FATHERS' of the Community would be surprised at the attention the EEC gives to women's affairs. The Treaty makes only one direct reference to women. Article 119 lays down that from the beginning member states should give effect to 'the principle that men and women should receive equal pay for equal work'. The French fought for the inclusion of this provision to eliminate distortions in the common market through different rates of pay for male and female workers doing the same work. On the basis of this article and others which empower the Community to improve the employment prospects of workers and harmonise social security legislation, an impressive range of measures has developed to redress the traditional inequalities faced by women in the labour market. The prominence of women's affairs when other issues have languished is in part due to the impact of the women's movement and in part to the

154

commitment and imagination of those responsible for social affairs in the Commission.

The Six agreed to the progressive removal of differentials in men's and women's pay for the same work and to their elimination by 1964. This had an effect on women's pay in public employment but loopholes were found which seemed to exempt the private sector, and the need for a Community directive on equal pay became obvious. During the late 1960s and early 1970s, the equal pay issue formed part of a wider debate about giving the Community a 'human face'. In 1972 the heads of government pledged to adopt a vigorous social policy to accompany the move towards economic union. In 1973 the Commission responded with a social action programme, which, among other things, proposed equal rights for women in the labour market. This programme, adopted by the Council in 1974, consisted of a series of far-reaching directives affecting women's rights in employment. Patrick Hillery, then Commissioner for Social Affairs, was responsible for the programme and its implementation.

The first of the directives was agreed by the Council in February 1975, and member states were obliged to implement it by February 1976 at the latest. It provided that women workers doing the same or similar work or work of equal value to men in all sectors of the economy should receive equal pay; that legal means of redress for women who were discriminated against be provided and that governments repeal all regulations or administrative provisions detrimental to working women. The directive was given added urgency by the decision of the Court of Justice in 1975 to uphold the case brought by a Belgian air-steward against Sabena airlines for paying her less than her male colleagues.

The application of this directive in Ireland provoked the first major public controversy about the Community. In 1971 the Council for the Status of Women had recommended that equal pay be phased in during the 1970s, and the programme of the national coalition government in 1973 included a commitment to equal pay, but little was done in practice to narrow the gap between men's and women's pay. The government, anticipating the directive on equal pay, passed the Anti-Discrimination (Pay) Act in 1974 which was to take effect in December 1975. As the date of introduction drew closer, the government came under pressure from employer organisations and one trade union which claimed that implementation of the directive would cost £40 million and cause 7,000 job losses in the leather and footwear industry. Liam Cosgrave's government prepared legislation to amend the 1974 Act postponing equal pay and applied to the Commission for a two-year derogation from the directive. When it came to a vote at the Commission, Dr Hillery, acting as an independent commissioner and as the person responsible for proposing the directive, voted against derogation. Minister for Finance Richie Ryan expressed the government's annoyance when he described Dr Hillery's action as 'the irresponsible antics of the Fianna Fáil-appointed Commissioner' and promptly requested financial assistance from the Commission to implement equal pay. The Commission refused to meet the cost of implementing the directive but softened the blow by agreeing to increase regional and social funds for Ireland.

In 1976 a second important directive was agreed concerning equal treatment for men and women workers. The government passed the Employment Equality Act in 1977 to give effect to the directive. The Act prohibits discrimination on grounds of sex or marital status in recruitment for employment, in training or conditions of employment or in opportunities for promotion. It also outlaws discriminatory job advertisements in the public press and media. Going beyond the minimum requirement of the directive, the Act also established an Employment Equality Agency to ensure compliance with the Act and with equal pay legislation and to promote equal opportunities in employment between the sexes. The Agency has the power to hold formal investigations and can seek High Court injunctions in cases of persistent discrimination. The Act gives Ireland a more effective means of enforcing equality legislation than most member states. One less well-understood implication of the Act is that men can no longer be discriminated against in jobs which have been traditionally the preserve of women - as secretaries, air-stewards, nurses.

The third directive agreed in November 1978 obliges member states to eliminate all discrimination based on sex or marital status in state social security schemes by 1985. The main group affected are married women who, since the introduction of social security, have been entitled to fewer and lower levels of benefit than single women or married men. The Commission has plans to follow up this directive with a regulation to outlaw discrimination in occupational social security schemes, particularly different pension and invalidity rules for men and women. The regulation will be directly binding on individual firms and will not require legislation by the Oireachtas.

What effect have these directives had on female employment? In 1981 the Commission issued a review report in which it found that appreciable progress had been made in law but that in practice the recession had resulted in job losses for women. The gap between men's and women's earnings, which had begun to narrow, is widening again. The Commission has also had to remind member states of their obligations under the directives. In 1980 the Commission warned Ireland that exclusions in the Employment Equality Act, excluding men from training as midwives and prohibiting mixed nursing of psychiatric patients, contravened the directive. The government has since removed these anomalies. In 1983 a spokeswoman for the Commission said that the system of recruiting women into the Gardai was under scrutiny because it may be too restrictive and discriminate against women.

Apart from these directives, the Commission has used other means at its disposal to promote the equality of women. In 1978 a special section of the social fund was made available to help solve problems specific to women in the job market. The fund provides assistance for operations which encourage the employment of women over twenty-five who wish to take up a job for the first time, to find a new job after redundancy or who wish to go back to work after a long absence. Ireland did not benefit at all from this special section until 1981 when AnCO ran three courses specially for women. The Irish share of these funds is still small - only 2% in 1982 compared with 57% for Germany and 23% for France. But of all Community operations financed from the social fund in 1982 about one-third of the beneficiaries were women, compared to 5% in 1974. (In Ireland, the Department of Labour is responsible for submissions for assistance to the social fund, while AnCO is the agency which organises most of the courses assisted by the fund.)

A further initiative in the Community's campaign on behalf of women is the Community action programme for 1982-85, taken primarily in response to a report passed by the European Parliament in 1981. An Advisory Committee on Equal Opportunities for Women and Men was set up and new directives drafted to promote equal opportunities for self-employed women and women employed in agriculture, and to provide for a system of leave for parental and family reasons.

The draft directive on equal treatment in self-employed occupations aims at removing inequalities - the absence of social security and opportunities for training. If passed, women working in family businesses would be recognised as equal partners in law and in professional or trade organisations. Women setting up in business on their own would have equal opportunities to train and access to credit facilities and professional bodies. Women entrepreneurs setting up in traditionally male sectors such as construction would be given a premium as a financial incentive to enter these sectors. The proposed directive on parental and family leave would allow both parents, whether married or not, to take paid leave after the birth of a child or to look after a sick relative. The main obstacle to the implementation of these directives is the cost. The action programme also emphasises the need to prepare women for jobs in the new 'microchip' technologies and to encourage men to share in domestic and family responsibilities.

The Women's Bureau in the Social Affairs Directorate-General of the Commission reviews all Community policies which affect women, informs women of their rights and how to take advantage of their legal and financial entitlements. It produces a monthly magazine *Women in Europe* and keeps up pressure for greater recognition of women's rights. In 1980 the Council of Education Ministers drew attention to the need to eliminate stereotyped images of the roles of the two sexes in educational material and in teaching. It encouraged young women to consider a wider range of career choices. The Commission is carrying out studies on the impact of co-education on the education of girls, ways of countering traditional prejudices and of making girls more aware of employment opportunities. In Ireland the Employment Equality Agency initiated a major research survey on schooling and sex roles in Irish education which detailed how girls' education reduces their career choices and highlighted the need for action to ensure equality of provision in education for boys and girls.

To what extent have the Community institutions lived up to these aspirations for women? The record is not so impressive. There has not yet been a woman commissioner or judge. There has been only one female advocate general. Of women employed in the Community, the vast majority are secretaries. No woman holds a post in the top spot of director general, and in the upper echelons of the bureaucrat system there are only six women competing with about five hundred male colleagues. The Commission is aware of the problem and in late 1983 Mr Burke, Commissioner for Personnel, announced an action programme to promote equality between male and female staff in the organisation.

The position of women in the Parliament is stronger. Of the 343 members, seventy are women, a larger proportion than in any national parliament. Two Irish women have been members of Parliament - Sile de Valera and Eileen Desmond. The first president of the directly elected Parliament was the French MEP, Simone Veil. Soon after the new Parliament assembled, an ad hoc committee of twenty-five women and ten men - but without Irish participation - was set up to report on the women's situation in the Community.

The report of that committee and a fifty-five point resolution were debated in Parliament in February 1981. The report called for the full implementation of Community legislation with a recommendation that the Commission should not pay regional and social funds to any government which was dragging its feet on the implementation of equal treatment and women's rights. It also called for a fundamental redistribution of work between men and women inside and outside the home; shorter and more flexible working hours; the same working and social conditions for part-time as for full-time workers; better vocational training for women to equip them for the new technologies and the harmonisation of national laws on maternity and paternity leave. It paid particular attention to the needs of

158

women in family businesses and agriculture. Many of its recommendations are reflected in the Commission's action programme for 1982-85.

Controversially, the Committee went on to urge that all EEC countries should provide contraception and abortion services for women, even though this was outside the Community's competence. Dr Dermot Ryan, Archbishop of Dublin, was so alarmed at the recommendations that he called a press conference at which he said that if there were a directive enforcing abortion throughout the Community the Irish people might have to decide to withdraw from the EEC. This brought an immediate response from Gaston Thorn, President of the Commission, who said that the Parliament had gone beyond its competence in discussing contraception and abortion and emphasised that the Treaty gives the Community no power to make laws on abortion. While it was politely suggested to Dr Ryan that he had misunderstood the nature of the Community and the limitation on its powers to act, the incident in retrospect can be seen as an opening shot in the campaign which led to the 1983 referendum to amend the Constitution guaranteeing the right to life of the unborn.

Women in the Community number 130 million or 51.6% of the total population. In the mid-1970s they accounted for 36% of persons employed in the Community but the effect of the prolonged recession and changing technology has actually reduced women's share of jobs. Community policies which were designed to encourage women to play a greater role in an expanding job market have in effect been helping women to hold onto their share in a declining market. Nor has equality legislation helped all women to the same extent. It has been of greater benefit to women in well-paid jobs who are aware of their rights than to the lower paid in segregated jobs.

These, and many more points about the situation of women in Europe were highlighted in a report of a committee of the European parliament, published in 1984. In debating the report, the Parliament agreed, to the surprise of many commentators, to a socialist resolution calling for a reduction in the working week to 35 hours to create more jobs for women.

As far as Ireland is concerned, the Community has brought about changes in employment practices which might otherwise have taken decades to achieve. Irish women have the Community to thank for the removal of the marriage bar in employment, the introduction of maternity leave, greater opportunities to train at a skilled trade, protection against dismissal on pregnancy, the disappearance of advertisements specifying the sex of an applicant for a job and greater equality in the social welfare code. After farmers, Irish women in employment have probably benefited most from entry to the EEC.

20
The Consumer, the Environment and Culture

REDUCING THE NOISE of lawnmowers, protecting the Irish wintering quarters of the Greenland white-fronted goose and sponsoring studies in the art of gardening are not activities immediately identifiable with the EEC. But in each of these cases the Community has a policy or proposal of interest to the consumer and to those who care about the environment and the cultural heritage of member states. Even without a specific mandate in the Treaty, the Commission has acted to strengthen these aspects of the 'human face' of the Community. Progress has been slow because each proposal must have the unanimous agreement of member states in the Council of Ministers.

THE CONSUMER

One of the earliest direct benefits to the consumer of the common market was a wider choice of goods and services and greater protection from unfair trading practices which push up the price of goods. By the 1970s these were considered insufficient protection for the consumer and in 1975 the Council of Ministers adopted a consumer information and protection programme guaranteeing consumers the right to safeguards for health and safety, to redress for damage caused by faulty articles, to information and education and to be consulted about policies. Richard Burke, in his first period as commissioner, was responsible for this ambitious programme. The prolonged recession reduced the willingness of member states to agree to the implementation of its provisions. Proposals drafted by Mr Burke have yet to be approved by the Council of Ministers.

In directives harmonising the law and practices of member states to ensure free circulation of goods, the Commission sought to guarantee the best health and safety protection for consumers. This has usually meant adjusting 'up' to the best practice in member states rather than settling for the lowest common denominator. Consumers in countries such as Ireland with few legal safeguards for the consumer have benefited by this raising of standards. The Community nudged Ireland into adopting two important pieces of legislation; the Consumer Information Act 1978 and the Sale of Goods and Supply of Services Act 1979. Under the former, a director of Consumer affairs was appointed to ensure that information supplied to consumers in the advertising, promotion and sale of goods and services is accurate. A Consumer Advisory Council was set up by the minister for industry and commerce to advise on legislation and consumer protection.

ENVIRONMENT POLICY

The Community's concern with protecting the environment in the early 1970s reflected growing alarm at international and national level that industrial and agricultural growth would destroy the ecological balance which supported life on the planet. Pollution from chemicals and gases threatened the quality of air in cities and of water in rivers, lakes and seas. Rachel Carson's book *Silent Spring* drew attention in 1962 to the way modern agriculture was driving wildlife out of the countryside. The oil spillage on the south coast of England from the *Torrey Canyon* in 1967 brought home to millions the dangers posed to amenities by industrialisation.

In 1973 the Council of Ministers agreed to an action programme which committed member states to recognising the environment as a precious resource. The action programme initiated directives on water and air pollution, the management of wastes and the protection of wildlife and habitats. The most important of these directives set limits for levels of smoke, sulphur dioxide and lead in the air, controlled the emissions from motor vehicles, set standards for different kinds of drinking and bathing water, controlled the noise of aeroplanes and cars and laid down guidelines for the protection of wild birds. A draft directive on reducing the noise of household appliances, including lawnmowers, is under discussion. In 1981 the Council agreed a regulation banning certain whale imports to discourage the extermination of this threatened species and in 1983 disgust at the cruelty of seal culling encouraged the Community to ban the import of products derived from seal pups.

Ireland has not received such attempts to protect the environment with much enthusiasm. Article 3 of the 1979 directive on bird conservation, for example, obliges member states to take any measures necessary to preserve a sufficient diversity and area of habitat for all the species of wild birds to which the directive applies. According to conservation expert John Temple Lang, no steps had been taken in Ireland by April 1983 to implement this clause. Neither has the government met a further obligation to supply the Commission with a list of the areas it intends to designate as wetlands of international importance or of other areas subject to habitat protection. Since Ireland is internationally important as a place where sea-birds and waterfowl winter, including the rare Greenland white-fronted goose, this lethargy is hard to understand. Ireland has only fifteen nature reserves, four national parks and only two areas totally protected from development. In Northern Ireland, one-fifth of the size of the Republic, there are over sixty nature reserves, forty-four areas of scientific interest and many more areas owned by the National Trust.

There has been some resistance to the suggestion from members of the European Parliament that some of Ireland's bogs, particularly the raised bogs of the midlands, be preserved for posterity. West Germany, Denmark, Italy and the Netherlands exhausted the bulk of their bogs at a time when little thought was given to conservation. Some of the Irish bogs are the best examples of their type remaining in western Europe and they support plants and insects which cannot be found anywhere else. While Irish people may take their bogs for granted, conservationists in other member states see them as a rich asset.

The heads of government at the European Council meeting in Stuttgart in 1983 reaffirmed their commitment to the 'urgent necessity of accelerating and reinforcing action, at national, Community and international level aimed at combatting the pollution of the environment'. While this statement helps the Commission press for more action in the priority areas of air pollution, waste management and the protection of the seas, it will not ensure that the agricultural and industrial interests which oppose more stringent controls will be overcome. The Electricity Supply Board announced its opposition on grounds of cost to a proposed directive to ban emissions of 'acid rain' which can destroy forests. Farmers oppose any further restrictions on the disposal of slurry and silage effluent while many fishermen fight attempts to preserve dwindling stocks of salmon. The principle which the Commission would like to see accepted is that protecting the environment is just as essential a part of good management as making profits - but the contamination of north-Dublin water supplies with phenol, of Ballyshannon's water with slurry, the poisoning of a Cork river with cyanide suggest that many people in Ireland remain unconvinced.

CULTURE

The cry of 'free trade in cultural goods' is unlikely to arouse much enthusiasm among the citizens of member states but behind it lies the important objective of uniting the peoples of Europe and promoting their social development. Restrictive national rules on the movements of artists (cultural workers!), on copyrights, royalties and the sale of works of art interfere with this objective as well as breaching the rules of the common market.

The Commission would like to see freelance artists covered by social security and the irregularity of their earnings taken into account for tax purposes. It has a draft directive prepared which would reduce VAT payments on art sales. The European social fund is empowered to support national programmes for the training of artists and the European regional fund can aid projects to support regional and minority cultures, many vacancies exist throughout the Community for orchestra players and creative craftworkers. Young musicians in Siena and Dublin and violin-makers in Cremona have received grants from the EEC and the Community also funds a youth orchestra with members drawn from all member states. The Community also gives fifty grants a year for the study of conservation and restoration at Louvain, Munich, Rome and Venice. Grants are given to architects, town-planners, specialised craftworkers, gardeners and persons interested in the preservation of cultural heritage. A small start has been made to protect historic architecture; the conservation of the famous hop house at the Guinness brewery in Dublin is being assisted by the Community.

The Community carefully avoids any suggestion of 'harmonising' the cultures of member states. Member states may be united by a common history and European identity but they are divided by language and cultural diversity. Even within member states there are cleavages of language and culture. As long as member states jealously guard their independence in this field, the Community's cultural activities will be limited to removing market restrictions and topping up national and regional efforts.

21
Northern Ireland

'WHAT WILL YOU HAVE?' asked Ireland's Foreign Minister, Brian Lenihan.

'An orange juice, please,' replied the Rev Ian Paisley, one of Northern Ireland's three members of the European Parliament.

'Done,' said Mr Lenihan, concluding his round.

The scene was the bar of the European Parliament in Strasbourg where Lenihan had been talking to journalists about the decision of the Parliament to reject the 1980 budget. Spotting the SDLP leader, John Hume, Lenihan moved across the room to have a quiet word with the Derryman, when in bounced the Reverend Ian. Immediately, Hume introduced them, and all three appeared to have a good banter going between them. Such an informal gathering could not take place in Dublin or Belfast - but it happened in Strasbourg.

The common market may still be unpopular in Northern Ireland but the European Parliament has provided a 'forum' to make the North's three MEPs - Paisley, Hume and the Official Unionist, John Taylor - more populist, if not popular, figures. These three hold a unique importance in European politics far beyond their small number in a 434-member Parliament, as they represent the one place within the Community where war is disrupting political and social life. Northern Ireland confronts the Community with the challenge of reconciling Ireland and Britain in the way that it ended the Franco-German enmity.

Unlike the Republic, Northern Ireland does not send politicians to take part in the Council of Ministers, nor has a Northerner been appointed a member of the Commission or of the European Court of Justice. As a region of the United Kingdom, Northern Ireland's interests in Europe are handled by the Westminster government and by the British permanent representation in Brussels. Northern Ireland's entry into the Community coincided with direct rule, so that while the Republic was able to throw itself with fervour into being a good European the North was absorbed by the traumas of British rule, the escalation of the IRA campaign, the Sunningdale agreement on power-sharing and its subsequent overthrow by the Ulster workers' strike. Yet, to the surprise of many commentators, the North voted narrowly in favour of continued EEC membership in the 1975 referendum.

ANATOMY

Northern Ireland has a population of 1.5 million compared to the Republic's 3.5 million. It has a Protestant majority, and a Catholic minority estimated at 40% of the population. With 10% of production based on agriculture, Northern Ireland has a higher dependence on farming than other UK regions. As in the Republic, farm incomes rose in the early 1970s, then fell sharply between 1978 and 1980 and later improved. In the past decade pig numbers fell by about 40% and poultry by about 20% as a result of Community restrictions on cheap imports of cereals from North America. Beef and dairy farming are the main sectors of the agricultural economy. About 20% of the labour force is involved directly or indirectly in agriculture. The farming organisations reflect inherited denominational differences: the Ulster Farmers' Union representing mainly Protestant dairy farmers, and the Northern Ireland Agricultural Producers representing the poorer Catholic hill farmers.

Northern Ireland is the fifth poorest region in the Community after the Republic, southern Italy, Sardinia and Greece. Income per head is only 77% of the UK average. Unemployment is running at 22% but is higher in Catholic areas west of the Bann and is above 50% of the adult male working population in west Belfast. In the past decade jobs in traditional manufacturing industries have dropped from 180,000 to 100,000. Shipbuilding, textiles and man-made fibre industries have been hit badly

Table 8

European Community Grants and Loans (Commitments) in Favour of Northern Ireland 1973-1983 (£ millions)

Grants	1973	1974	1975	1976	1977	1978	1979	1980	1981	1982	1973-83
Agricultural fund	1,743	2,198	2,986	1,693	2,199	1,086	2,394	2,498	2,689	2,429	21,915
Regional fund	–	–	7,750	7,205	9,370	14,230	27,840	19,230	28,220	23,420	139,265
Social fund	4,080	4,950	4,740	13,580	9,570	16,400	24,229	26,932	30,022	50,117	184,620
Energy measures (£ 000's)	–	–	–	–	36	6	63	–	–	–	105
Total grants	5,823	7,148	15,476	22,478	21,175	31,722	54,526	48,660	60,931	75,966	345,905
Loans											
European Investment Bank	–	2,500	167	–	18,500	–	52,300	49,240	5,770	223	128,700
United Kingdom supplementary measures (claimed on behalf of Northern Ireland)	–	–	–	–	–	–	–	–	94,200	117,548	211,748
Total grants and loans	5,823	9,648	15,643	22,478	39,675	31,722	106,826	97,900	160,901	193,737	686,353

Grand total: grants, loans and United Kingdom supplementary measures claimed on behalf of Northern Ireland: £686,353,000.

by the recession, and violence has made it more difficult to attract new investments.

Some 40% of the North's total public expenditure, including security, is paid by British taxpayers: in 1984 the contribution to Northern Ireland was £1.5 billion. This British contribution is massive compared to the £686 million in grants and loans from the Community to the North between 1973 and 1983 (see Table 8). The size of its contribution has encouraged the British government to regard Community aid to Northern Ireland as a reimbursement for, rather than an addition to, monies spent.

Along with the Republic, the North is one of the five regions which qualify for high priority aid from the regional fund, and it benefits from the extra 10% assistance from the social fund. Like the Republic, Northern Ireland has availed of preferential loans from the European Investment Bank, having the distinction of obtaining the first interest rate subsidy on a £33 million loan for the Kilroot power station. The guidance section of the farm fund provided over £21 million for farmers in Northern Ireland, but the British government wants to broaden the number of farmers eligible for grants and development programmes by extending the 'less favoured areas' from 45% to 70% of the total agricultural land area. The Council of Ministers adopted a five-year cross-border project with the Republic in June 1981 in which Northern Ireland obtained £4.5 million from the non-quota section of the regional fund for the development of tourism, small industries and craft industries, and for communications in the local council areas between Newry and Mourne in the east and Derry in the West. EEC financial support was made available to sponsor joint studies on transport and communications in Derry-Donegal, on drainage in the Armagh-Louth area and for a study of the Erne catchment area. A series of nine reports on cross-border issues was financed by the Community for the Cooperation North organisation. Early in 1984 the EEC's Economic and Social Committee published a report on Irish border areas proposing a range of measures costing £1 billion. In addition, an improved Newry-Dundalk road is being planned with EEC funding.

IMPACT

With the collapse in 1974 of the power-sharing executive and assembly, the North lost its one representative, Rafton Pounder, in the old nominated European Parliament. Thus, the 1979 direct elections gave the North a chance to get onto the European stage. It was due to the efforts of Garret FitzGerald, the Republic's Foreign Minister, that the Council of Ministers approved three seats for Northern Ireland to be contested as a single constituency on the proportional representation system rather than the first-past-the-post system used elsewhere in Britain. As intended, this enabled John Hume to take a seat in Strasbourg along with Ian Paisley and John Taylor. There, a partnership of a remarkable kind developed among the three Northern MEPs on matters of economic interest to Northern Ireland. The initiative was taken by Hume who as an adviser to Commissioner Richard Burke's cabinet was well acquainted with the workings of the EEC. He tabled a resolution in Parliament calling on the Commission to analyse Northern Ireland's problems in the light of Community membership and to put forward proposals on how additional Community resources might be made available to help solve these problems. This motion was supported by the Northern Ireland Office in London, which, in a briefing to UK members of the European Parliament, commented: 'A new or greater role for the use of Community funds in Northern Ireland would be welcome both for their intrinsic benefits and because they would help to reduce the imbalance between the United Kingdom's payments to the EEC and its receipts.'

The task of preparing a report was assigned by the Parliament's Regional Affairs Committee to a French Liberal, Simone Martin, who visited the North in September 1980. Shortly afterwards, attention switched to Commissioner Richard Burke, who, in a speech to Belfast City Council, disclosed that at the request of the Commission, the British government was considering spending about £100 million of Community money on Belfast over a four or five-year period. This speech was countered by Northern Ireland Secretary Humphrey Atkins who said that there was 'no crock of gold in Brussels waiting to be picked up for the asking.' Despite this disavowal, Mr Burke opened a debate about the Community's role in Northern Ireland and created public interest in the question of whether or not the British government was 'pocketing' money which the Commission would prefer to be 'additional' to British spending in Northern Ireland.

Attention returned to Parliament where in June 1981 Mme Martin's report was endorsed. The report accepted that Northern Ireland should be given special attention and called on the Commission to prepare a report on Community aid to the North. It also questioned the British government's handling of EEC grants to Northern Ireland, deploring 'the fact that this aid is often kept by the government to defray its own expenditure in Northern Ireland instead of being paid over as additional outlay.' The Martin report concluded that 'compliance with the principle of additionality is the key to genuine economic and social assistance from the Community for Northern Ireland.'

The Martin report inspired the Commission - which set up a task force of commissioners to discuss Northern Ireland matters - to propose a 1982 budget allocation of £16 million as Community aid for Belfast housing with a unique provision in the legal arrangements requiring proof of its genuine additionality. But the proposal was blocked by West Germany which did not wish to create a precedent for others. However, the special economic and social problems of Belfast were gaining recognition in the Community. Along with Naples, Belfast was chosen to pioneer the integrated operations plan, an urban renewal project. In Belfast, housing, transport, industrial infrastructure and vocational training were identified as the areas for attention. The cost of the latter three areas was £250 million. It is hoped that the £70 million Community aid for Belfast agreed by the Council in 1983 for a three-year period will enable the British government to release funds for housing.

Meanwhile, developments in Anglo-Irish relations tested the alliance of the three Northern MEPs. The talks between Irish and British Prime Ministers Charles Haughey and Margaret Thatcher on the future of Northern Ireland enraged loyalist opinion - but the special relationship between the two leaders did not last long, especially when Haughey ended his support for EEC sanctions against Argentina following the sinking by the British navy of the Argentinian battleship, the *Belgrano*. Within Northern Ireland the death of ten H Block hunger strikers paved the way for the electoral rise of Provisional Sinn Fein. Also, John Hume's decision not to enter a restored Assembly left him more isolated from Paisley and Taylor, both of whom attended Stormont.

In this predicament Hume displayed outstanding political skill by launching a new initiative that brought Northern Ireland to the centre of the activities of the European Parliament. Along with others, he persuaded Parliament to undertake a comprehensive inquiry into the situation in Northern Ireland, despite the opposition of Mrs Thatcher to the fact that the study would examine internal and political security and cross-border cooperation. The task of drawing up the report was assigned by the Political Affairs Committee to a Danish Liberal, Niels Haagerup. Outside the scope of investigation was the constitutional position of Northern Ireland. Haagerup's aim was to inform Europeans of the Northern Ireland problem and to suggest ways in which the Community might assist that troubled area.

The Haagerup report urged the British and Irish governments to back power-sharing in Northern Ireland. Although it dismissed the possibility of a unitary Irish state in the foreseeable future, it urged the British and Irish governments to set up a joint Anglo-Irish parliamentary body with representatives from Westminster and the Dáil. The main economic proposal was for the Community to present 'an integrated plan for a major contribution to the development of Northern Ireland.' In Haagerup's view 'the European Parliament has assumed a large degree of responsibility for the economic and social development of Northern Ireland by deciding to draw up a report on the whole problem of Northern Ireland. This is a unique decision.' Determined to nail the Parliament to that responsibility, Haagerup concluded that the report must be executed not just by pious declarations of intent but by concrete undertakings and projects in addition to those already underway. This should be done in the context of 'the comprehensive Irish-British understanding, which remains the core of and the clue to any lasting improvement of the situation in Northern Ireland.'

The Haagerup report was adopted by the European Parliament on 29 March 1984 by 124 votes to three. With one exception, the Conservative group, primarily composed of British Conservatives, abstained, although its spokesperson, Lady Elles, commended the report as balanced and the Derry-born Sir Frederick Catherwood described it as excellent. The three opponents were Paisley, Taylor and the Independent Republican, Neil Blaney. The Parliament's adoption of the report was welcomed by Irish Foreign Minister Peter Barry, as offering new hope to the people of both traditions in the North. The report's emphasis on increased cooperation by the Irish and British governments was seen by Mr Barry as helpful, coming so soon after the endorsement by President Ronald Reagan of the aims of the New Ireland Forum.

The Commission responded to the report by reconvening the special committee of commissioners to examine how the Community could increase economic aid to Northern Ireland.

Also, the position of Northern Ireland was raised in the negotiations on the controversial super-levy on surplus milk production. Following Dr FitzGerald's walk-out from the Brussels meeting of heads of government, the British government, in an apparent gesture of conciliation, announced that it would expect that any special deal for the Republic on the super-levy would apply also to Northern Ireland. This posed something of a dilemma for the Dublin government since the Irish case for special treatment rested on the gap between average milk yields in Ireland and the Community. Milk yields per cow in Northern Ireland, however, are close to the EEC average. As part of the compromise package agreed after marathon discussions, Northern Ireland was permitted an additional 65,000 tonnes of milk, an increase of 6% on levels agreed for the other partners. However, this pales into insignificance beside the increase of 20% allowed to farmers in the Republic and is estimated to amount to as much as £20 million in lost income to Northern farmers. Nor is Northern Ireland included in the guarantee given to Dublin that Irish farmers would receive priority if additional production were allowed. The 'clawback' on the UK variable premium on beef exports means that Northern beef farmers no

170

longer enjoy a price advantage over producers from other member states in EEC and world markets. John Hume justifiably described the farm package as a disaster for Northern agriculture, and called for a cross-border agricultural regime to protect the interests of the dairy industry in the Republic and Northern Ireland.

The Community may not have helped resolve the problems of Northern Ireland in the way many hoped on accession. Nonetheless it has provided an invaluable forum for the leaders of the two traditions in the North to work together and has increased contact between Southern politicians and their northern counterparts. The decision of Provisional Sinn Fein to contest the European Parliamentary elections of June 1984 and to take their seats if elected, illustrates the symbolic importance of the Parliament to the Northern minority. The strong bargaining power of Dublin within the EEC is a source of envy to the North which must rely on British representation of their interests in Brussels. As the super-levy negotiations showed, such representation is not always wholehearted. The Haagerup report is a sign that the problems of Northern Ireland can no longer be seen purely as domestic concerns of the UK, nor as bilateral issues between the British and Irish governments. A Community dedicated to the peaceful unification of its peoples cannot succeed while conflict in Northern Ireland continues.

22
Administration and Politics

Taoiseach Jack Lynch and Michael O'Kennedy preside over a meeting of the European Council.

THE WHITE PAPERS of 1970 and 1972, detailing the implications of membership of the EEC, made no reference to the civil service. Yet the civil service, particularly the Department of Finance, could be said to have discovered the EEC as far as Ireland is concerned. It is arguable that the people whose lives have been most changed by membership are officials of the Departments of Agriculture, Foreign Affairs, Finance and Labour. Accession added a new dimension to the work of these departments and their staff. It is their responsibility to shape EEC policy in Brussels and to ensure that Community decisions are implemented. The relatively small size of the Commission precludes it from administering policies in each member state. It keeps a watching brief to ensure compliance, leaving the job of adapting domestic law and administration to the bureaucracies of the ten member states.

Because of the importance of the common agricultural policy, the major burden of administration has fallen on the Department of Agriculture. That Department is responsible for administering the market price support and intervention system and the farm modernisation and disadvantaged areas schemes. Officials spend a great deal of time in Brussels attending meetings of management committees at the Commission or at Council working parties representing the Irish view when decisions are taken about the operation of the policy. In 1983 the number of meetings attended by officials of the Department was just under eight hundred, about three per working day! The number of attendances by officials was more than a thousand. Not surprisingly, the administrative staff of the Department has doubled since 1970, from sixty-two to 124.

Of the central coordinating Departments - Finance, Foreign Affairs, Public Service and the Taoiseach - the role of the Department of Foreign Affairs has been most radically altered by membership. A relatively unimportant ministry before membership, its status has been boosted by the importance in the Community of foreign affairs and of the presidency, the development of political cooperation and the growth of Ireland's relationship with the Third World. Dermot Scott has suggested that 'the essential element in the Department's evolution in the 1970s has been in its adaptation to multilateral diplomacy in economic affairs.' To cope with this increased workload, the administrative staff rose from forty-three to 110 between 1970 and 1981.

While the Department of Finance took the leading role in the negotiations before entry it was content after 1973 to let the Department of Foreign Affairs play the main coordinating role in Ireland's approach to the Community. Nonetheless, it retains control over financial and economic aspects of membership, excluding agriculture and the social fund. Among its principal Community responsibilities are the regional fund, loans from the European Investment Bank, the European monetary system, tax harmonisation and Ireland's contributions to the budget. Neither the structure of the Department nor the number of personnel were greatly changed by these additional responsibilities.

One of the preconditions of effective negotiations in Brussels is a coordinated national viewpoint. Community bargaining often involves trade-offs between one sector and another and national representatives must know in advance the strength of the cards they hold. Each member state coordinates instructions at a domestic level in order that ministers, permanent representatives and officials speak with a united voice in Brussels. The French have a highly centralised and bureaucratic system, the Danes a system of strong parliamentary supervision and the Germans have relaxed and informal arrangements. The main coordinating arrangement on EEC policy of the Irish government is the European Communities Committee, composed of the secretaries of the Departments of the Taoiseach, Agriculture, Finance, Trade and Industry and chaired by the secretary of the Department of Foreign Affairs. Meeting at least once a month, it has the job of formulating policy, establishing priorities and briefing the government on issues of major importance. The permanent representative - the Irish ambassador to the Community - attends its meetings to maintain links between Dublin and COREPER. Also, the small size of the Irish administrative system makes informal coordination possible at a lower level. Officials of different departments who travel to Brussels tend to know each other and may resolve differences on the plane from Dublin. A cabinet sub-committee dealing with EEC affairs was established shortly after Ireland joined the Community to coordinate EEC policy at ministerial level. It fell into disuse but was revived during the difficult negotiations on the super-levy.

Participation in the process of Community decision-making has posed one of the greatest challenges to the Irish public service since the Second World War. There is general agreement that Irish officials have acquitted themselves well when it comes to defending Irish interests round the table in Brussels. However, Joseph Lee has questioned the skill of Irish civil servants in choosing the ground on which to negotiate longer-term issues. Nor have Irish officials made a significant contribution to the resolution of the fundamental difficulties facing the Community. The lack of exposure of officials to a European background and the general limitations of Irish people in respect of foreign languages do pose problems. Although interpretation and translation are provided, much negotiation and debate takes place in corridors outside the formal meetings. Officials who can talk to their counterparts in their own language have a much greater chance of getting their point across than those who cannot. The lack of a European background may also contribute to the attitude that the Community exists to provide solutions to Irish problems, particularly in the form of financial handouts. But membership also involves a commitment to the ideals underlying the Community and towards their creative adaptation to the conditions of the 1980s.

SUPERVISING COMMUNITY ACTIVITIES

If the civil service has adapted successfully to membership, the political system has shown few signs of coming to terms with the new dimension of Community affairs. The Dáil and Seanad have not developed effective means of supervising the executive activities of government and this weakness extends to the executive activities of the Community. Apart from an obligation on the government to make a twice-yearly report to the

Oireachtas on developments in the European communities, no arrangements were made in the preparations for entry to strengthen the power of the Oireachtas in supervising Community laws in this country. Yet, section 3 of the European Communities Act 1972 empowered the government to amend statute law by regulation if necessary in order to meet the obligations of membership. This gave ministers extraordinarily wide powers to make legislation by delegation, using the constitutional amendment as justification. When the coalition government came into power in 1973 it amended the Act to provide for an Oireachtas Joint Committee on the Secondary Legislation of the European Communities. Regulations made under the parent Act cease to have statutory effect if within one year of their adoption, the Dáil and Seanad, acting on the recommendation of the Committee, pass resolutions to annul them.

Of the 227 sets of regulations made under the Act between January 1973 and December 1981, the Committee has recommended to the Dáil that two be annulled. However, the Dáil was dissolved before a vote was taken and the regulations remain in force. Also, the Committee recommended that the two statutory instruments to facilitate the free movement of dentists and nurses be annulled unless the minister for health gave an undertaking to amend them as recommended by the Committee. A compromise was reached. Furthermore, the Committee has criticised the practice of governments of amending major legislation such as the Companies Act 1963 by the use of statutory instruments.

The present Joint Committee is the fourth to be appointed, its predecessors dissolving on the same day as the Dáil by which they were appointed. The Committee is empowered to examine programmes for draft Community legislation, acts of the Council and Commission, and statutory instruments necessitated by membership of the Community. It may employ consultants to carry out research on its behalf. It is not empowered to examine non-statutory schemes such as the farm modernisation and disadvantaged areas schemes, nor the activities of political cooperation. A further limitation on the Committee's effectiveness is that officials giving evidence before it are debarred from raising questions of policy and must confine their answers to factual details. The Joint Committee had produced ninety-three reports by May 1981, a reflection of how hard members worked. Despite this industry, the Dáil and Seanad have shown little interest in debating such reports. It seems that the main impact of the Joint Committee has been to improve the drafting of statutory instruments in departments. Because of frequent changes of government, no reports were produced between the summer of 1981 and the end of 1983. The Oireachtas has also been slow to debate the twice-yearly reports of the government on developments in the European communities prepared by the Department of Foreign Affairs. The statements of the Taoiseach to the Dáil on the outcome of the European Council have generated greater enthusiasm among politicians. The high politics of the Community attract more attention than do the bread-and-butter issues covered by the Joint Committee and departmental reports.

Other countries have more active parliamentary supervision of Community activity. The Danish, Dutch and Germans have the most effective parliamentary committees. These committees not only have the function of supervising Community activity but they also contribute actively to government policy on European matters. It is not unusual for Danish ministers in Brussels to find themselves unable to reach agreement with their fellow Council members because they have no mandate from the powerful Market Relations Committee of the Danish parliament.

MEDIA AND INTEREST GROUPS

The standard of coverage of day-to-day Community issues in the Irish media is good, reflecting the importance of Community activity to so many aspects of Irish life. The longer-term issues affecting Community development are not so well covered or explained. There are still widespread misconceptions about the role of the Community and, particularly, the extent of its powers under the Treaty.

Perhaps the most vocal critique of Community activity and of government EEC policy comes from the groups representing the major interests affected by membership - the Irish Farmers' Association, the Federated Union of Employers, the Confederation of Irish Industry, the Irish Congress of Trade Unions and the Irish Fishermen's Organisation. Many of these organisations have an intimate knowledge of the workings of the Community and are well placed to influence government policy on issues which affect them. By their nature they are not directly concerned with the wider issues of European integration. It is the Irish Council of the European Movement which aims to promote greater integration between member states by providing a forum for those interested in airing ideas and influencing people.

23
The Balance Sheet

The Berlaymont, star-shaped home of the Commission, with the headquarters of the
Council on the left.

MANY OF THE EFFECTS of Irish membership of the EEC cannot be quantified.
Patrick Keatinge has commented that 'Membership . . . represented a
qualitative change in the way in which Ireland interacted with the world.'
Partnership in one of the major economic powers has increased Ireland's
standing in the world far beyond that of other small dependent nations.
Before accession, Ireland's 'external relations' were dominated by proximity
to and dependence on Britain. Joining the Community provided the country
with an opportunity to develop 'foreign' policies on a wide range of issues
and to influence world events.

Equally difficult to quantify is the way in which membership has changed
Irish people's lives. Individuals can now move freely throughout the
Community to work or search for a job without losing their own or their
dependents' right to social security. The Community's stance on equal

pay and equality of opportunity between men and women in relation to employment were major steps forward in Irish women's struggle for recognition in the work place. And how does one measure the political impact on the 60% of the electorate who voted in the world's first direct elections to a multinational parliament in 1979?

Most attention is understandably focused on the quantifiable effects of membership such as increases in the income of the farming community, grants from the regional and social funds and loans from the European Investment Bank. Table 4 shows how much the country has benefited financially from membership between 1973 and 1983. The income Ireland received greatly exceeded its contributions to the Community. If it had not been for this inflow of money into the economy following accession, the country would have been much more severely damaged by the 1973 recession and its aftermath. The optimistic expectations for agricultural markets and prices were realised, although a question mark now hangs over the future expansion of the Irish dairy industry. Membership opened up a large and lucrative market to Irish manufacturers and to firms attracted to Ireland by special incentives. Foreign firms which took advantage of such opportunities are now the main export earners in the country. Trade is no longer over-dependent on the British market.

On the debit side of the balance sheet, membership of the Community has brought problems of adaptation and redistribution. Many industries were unable to survive the combined effects of the removal of protective barriers to trade and prolonged recession. The extent to which farmers benefited financially from membership, in the absence of a consensus on how this new wealth ought to be taxed, led to antagonism between town and country. Within the farming community the larger farmers have benefited to a much greater extent than the smaller marginal farmers. Nor have higher EEC prices for agricultural goods had much effect on the level of gross agricultural output in the last ten years.

Despite the large financial transfers from the Community during the 1970s, the gap between Ireland and her partners on an index of gross domestic product per head widened during the period by a small margin. This occurred despite the fact that the Irish economy performed better than those of its partners. The income gap per head widened because the Irish population rose by 9.5%, a rate unequalled in any other EEC country in the 1970s. The Irish economy has to perform better than its neighbours and better than it did in the 1970s if the standard of living enjoyed by the population ten years ago is to be maintained. Table 9 ranks nine EEC countries on twelve socio-economic indicators. It shows that Ireland has had the highest population growth, birth rate and age dependency ratio of the nine; the largest proportion of persons employed in agriculture and the smallest employed in industry; the lowest gross domestic product (income) per worker and per head; the lowest number of cars and telephones per hundred inhabitants; and the second highest rate of unemployment. The table conveys the scale of the problems faced by this country and the challenge to the ideals of the EEC which commit it to 'reducing the differences existing between the various regions and backwardness of the less favoured regions'.

The twelve years of membership have had no obvious effect on Irish culture. There are more French, German and Dutch tourists visiting Ireland and more Irish people holiday on the continent but it is hard to know if tourism has a lasting impact, apart from directing the Irish palate to the delights of good food and wine. Irish folk music is popular in the

Table 9

Comparison between Nine EEC Member States: Twelve Socio-Economic Indicators

Indicator	Max.	Min.	Ireland's indicator	Ireland's ranking
Population growth (%) (1973-79)	+9.5	−1.1	9.5	1
Birth rate (1977)	20.8	9.5	20.8	1
Migration rate (1977)	+2.1	−0.8	2.1	1
Age dependency (1977)	0.73	0.49	0.73	1
Labour force dependence (1977)	1.88	1.09	1.80	3
Agricultural share of total employment (%) (1977)	21.7	2.9	21.7	1
Industry's share of total Unemployed rate (%) (1979)	45.0	32.4	32.4	9
Unemployed rate (%) (1977)	8.7	0.8	7.9	2
GDP per worker (EEC—9+100) EUA (1977)	146	60	60	9
GDP per head (EEC—9+100) EUA (1979)	141	51	51	9
Cars per 100 inhabitants (1977)	39.8	16.2	16.2	9
Telephone per 100 inhabitants (1977)	38.4	10.9	10.9	9

Source: From Tables 10, 11 and 18: The Socio-Economic Position of Ireland within the European Economic Community, NESC No. 58.

Netherlands, Denmark and Germany but our young people seem uninterested in the music of other member states, excluding Britain. Ireland remains culturally part of the Anglo-American world, despite the continued hold of the Roman Catholic Church and the Gaelic heritage. The low priority of spoken European languages in schools and universities reinforces Ireland's isolation from the continent and limits the job, cultural and recreational opportunities for young Irish people in the EEC.

And what of Ireland's image in the EEC? The answer may not be flattering to the national ego. Irish behaviour in the Community has probably been more constructive than the minimalism of Denmark or the obstructionism of the United Kingdom. But Ireland's 'Europeanism' has masked what Patrick Keatinge has called a 'persistent temptation to succumb to "green gaullism" and to put short term advantage before long term gain'. In Joseph Lee's view, the Brussels connection has 'reinforced the powerful sponger syndrome in the Irish value system'. The demand to be treated as a special case without making concessions in return has not enhanced the Irish image. The extent of the concessions made to Ireland on the question of the super-levy is not understood or appreciated by the general public. The controversies surrounding the appointment and departure of some Irish members of the Commission also raises questions about the importance attached to the Community and its institutions. To use neutrality as an excuse for refusing to discuss European defence mystifies our partners and suggests to them an ostrich-like attitude to the realities of power politics. More seriously, Ireland has not taken a lead in proposing new schemes for European union or strengthening the Community. On the contrary there are signs of growing indifference to a strong Community. It is not difficult to see why eight of the partners have difficulty in distinguishing Ireland's image from Britain's in the Community.

The advantage to Ireland of membership of the EEC is so great that it is surprising that this fact does not underlie attitudes and policies towards the Community. For Irish governments to allow the Community to be weakened or fall apart by failure to agree on solutions to the problems facing the Ten would be counter-productive, to say the least. As a small country Ireland has more to gain by compromise, following the rules and insisting that its larger partners do the same, than by short-sighted obstructionism. As one of the member states most dependent on trade and with a rapidly expanding population, Ireland needs to be part of a strong and united economic Community in Europe. Irish strategy should be to strengthen the Community and its own position within it even if this requires some sacrifice of short-term interest. A combination of idealism and realism is needed if the Community is to overcome the internal and external threats to its existence in a spirit worthy of its founders.

Euro-Information

The Commission's Irish offices at 39 Molesworth Street, Dublin 2, and at Windsor House, Bedford Street, Belfast BT2 7EG, provide an information service on all aspects of Community law, policies and policy proposals. The Dublin office has an excellent reference library which is open to the public from 9.30 to 13.00 and 14.00 to 17.30, Monday to Friday. The office has general and specialised films, sets of slides and video cassettes available for loan. Wall maps, posters and similar material relating to the Community are also available. A limited number of visits to the headquarters of the Community institutions for individuals or groups whose study or work involves them closely with the Community can be arranged each year.

REGULAR COMMUNITY PUBLICATIONS

The Official Journal Published in three series: 'L' which contains each law passed by the European Communities; 'C' containing information and notices, e.g. competitions to recruit staff; 'S' carrying announcements about public supply and works contracts in the Community and under association agreements with third countries.

Bulletin of the European Communities Reports on the activities of the Commission and the other Community institutions and is published eleven times a year.

European File A regular publication of the Information Directorate of the Commission explaining Community policies in brief.

General Report of the Activities of the European Communities An annual publication.

European Documentation An occasional series giving detailed information on particular policies.

European Economy A quarterly publication, including an annual economic report, with three supplements: *Economic Trends* - eleven issues a year; *Business Survey Results* - eleven issues a year; *Consumer Survey Results* - three issues a year.

Annual Reports on the Common Agricultural Policy, Competition and the Social Situation.

Community Report Monthly publication of the Irish office of the Commission, Dublin, available free of charge on request.

Eorascáil A short newsletter in Irish, published monthly by the Irish office of the Commission, Dublin, available free of charge on request.

Europe in Northern Ireland Regular publication of the European Commission office in Northern Ireland, available free of charge on request.

GOVERNMENT PUBLICATIONS

Developments in the European Communities Twice-yearly report by the Irish government to the Oireachtas, containing a record of all Community decisions, particularly as they affect Ireland.

SALES

All official European Communities and government publications can be purchased through the Government Publication Sales Office, Sun Alliance House, Molesworth Street, Dublin 2, tel. (01) 710309, or by post from Government Publications Postal Sales Office, St Martin's House, Waterloo Road, Dublin 4.

The Eurocrat's Who's Who

INSTITUTIONS AND ORGANISATIONS

Council of Ministers: Secretariat, Rue de la Loi 170, 1040 Brussels. Tel. 234 6111. *Secretary General* - Niels Ersboll.
Commission of the European Communities: Rue de la Loi 200, 1040 Brussels. Tel. 235 1111. *Secretary General* - Emile Noel.
Commission's Dublin Office: 39 Molesworth Street, Dublin 2. Tel. (01) 712244. *Director* - Conor Maguire. *Deputy Director* (Press Office and Publications) - Peter Doyle. *Head of Information* - Tim Kelly.
Commission's Office in Northern Ireland: Windsor House, 9/15 Bedford Street, Belfast. Tel. (084) 240708. *Head of Office* - Geoffrey Martin.
Stagiaire Applications: The Commission has a system of recruiting young graduates for six months work experience in Directorates General or in other branches of the Community. Stagiaires receive a grant which enables them to live comfortably and have the opportunity to participate in organised trips to Berlin, Strasbourg and Luxembourg. Applications should be made through the Commission offices in Dublin and Belfast.
European Parliament: Its three venues are - Palais de l'Europe, Strasbourg. Tel. 374001. Secretariat, Centre Européen, C.P. 1601, Luxembourg. Tel. 43001. 97-113 Rue Belliard, 1040 Brussels. Tel. 234 2111.
European Parliament Dublin Office: 43 Molesworth Street, Dublin 2. Tel. (01) 719100. *Head of Information* - Joe Fahy. *Assistant* - Dermot Scott.
European Court of Justice: Secretariat, Plateau de Kirchberg, Luxembourg. Tel. 43031. *Registrar* - Paul Heim.
Economic and Social Committee: Rue Ravenstein 2, 1000 Brussels. Tel. 512 3920. *Chairman* - Francois Ceyrac. *Secretary-General* - Roger Louet. *Irish members* - John Carroll, Henry Curlis, John Kenna, Donal Cashman, Sean Kelly, P.J. Loughrey, Patrick Murphy, Gordon Pearson, Tomas Roseingrave.
European Investment Bank: 100 Boulevard Konrad Adenauer, L-2950 Luxembourg. Tel. 43791. *President* - Yves Le Portz. *Vice President* - Noel Whelan.
European Court of Auditors: 20 Rue Aldringen, Luxembourg. Tel. 47731. *President* - Pierre Lelong. *Irish member* - Michael Murphy.
European Foundation for Living and Working Conditions: Loughlinstown House, Shankill, Co. Dublin. Tel. (01) 826888.
European Centre for the Development of Vocational Training: Bundesallee 22, D 1000 - Berlin 15. Tel. (16-49-30) 884120.
Permanent Representation of Ireland to the European Communities: Avenue Gailee 5, 1030 Brussels. Tel. (16322) 2180605 (telex no. (046) 26730). *Ambassador & Permanent Representative* - Andrew O'Rourke. *Deputy Permanent Representative* - John Swift.
Oireachtas Joint Committee on the Secondary Legislation of the European Communities: Leinster House, Dublin 2. Tel. (01) 789910. *Clerk* - Seamus Phelan. *Chairman* - Gerry Collins TD. *Dail members* - Sylvester Barrett, Mattie Brennan, Liam Burke, Hugh Conaghan, Cathal Coughlan, Brendan Daly, Dick Dowling, Bernard Durcan, Oliver J. Flanagan, Brendan Griffin, Maurice Manning, Donie Ormonde, Joe Walsh. *Senate members* - Jim Higgins, Richard Hourigan, Mick Lanigan, Charlie McDonald, Mary Robinson, Shane Ross, Michael Smith.

Advisory Council on Development Cooperation: 43 Fitzwilliam Square, Dublin 2. Tel. (01) 766552. *Chairwoman* - Helen O'Neill. *Executive Secretary* - Veronica Canning. Consists of thirty voluntary members appointed by the minister for foreign affairs for three years (renewable).

Department of Agriculture: Agriculture House, Dublin 2. Tel. (01) 789011. *Minister* - Austin Deasy TD. *Ministers of State* - Paddy Hegarty TD and Paul Connaughton TD. *Secretary* - Jim O'Mahony.
An Bord Bainne Cooperative Ltd.: (Irish Dairy Board), Grattan House, Lower Mount Street, Dublin 2. Tel. (01) 785788. *Managing Director* - Brian Joyce. *Public Relations Manager* - Pat McDonagh.
Coras Beostoic agus Feola: (Irish Livestock and Meat Board), Clanwilliam Court, Lower Mount Street, Dublin 2. Tel. (01) 685155. *Managing Director* - Dr Tony O'Sullivan.
Irish Cooperative Organisation Society Ltd.: 84 Merrion Square, Dublin 2. Tel. (01) 764783. *President* - John Barry. *Director General* - James Maloney. *Secretary* - Greg Tierney. ICOS is affiliated to COGECA - the General Committee for Agricultural Cooperation in the EEC, Rue de la Science 23/5, 1040 Brussels. Tel. (16322) 2303945.
Irish Creamery Milk Suppliers' Association: John Feely House, Upper Mallow Street, Limerick. Tel. (061) 314677. *President* - Sean Kelly. *General Secretary* - Donal Murphy.
Irish Farmers' Association: Irish Farm Centre, Naas Road, Bluebell, Dublin 12. Tel. (01) 501166. *President* - Joe Rea. *Deputy President* - Alan Gillis. *General Secretary* - Michael Berkery. *Chief Economist* - Con Lucey. *Press Officer* - Tony Gallagher. *Director of Brussels Office* - John Smith. Rue de la Science 23/5, 1040 Brussels. Tel. (16322) 2303137. The IFA is a member of the Community-wide lobby, COPA.
Irish Meat Exporters Association: Marine House, Clanwilliam Court, Dublin 2. Tel. (01) 760951. *Chief Executive* - Eugene Regan.

The EEC Banking Federation (Federation Bancaire de la CEE): Avenue de Tervuren 168, 1150 Brussels. Tel. (16322) 7628303. *Secretary General* - Paul Fabre. *Irish board members:* W.D. Finlay (*President*), Irish Bankers' Federation Director, Bank of Ireland, Lower Baggot Street, Dublin 2. Tel. (01) 785744. Niall Crowley (*Vice-President*).

CONGOOD (Confederation of Non-Governmental Organisations for Overseas Development): 32 Kildare Street, Dublin 2. Tel. (01) 762298. *Chairman* - Brian McKeown (Trocaire). *Member agencies:* Association of Missionary Societies, Christian Aid, Church of Ireland Bishops' Appeal, Comhlámh, Concern, Gorta, Irish Commission for Justice and Peace, Irish Council for Overseas Students, Irish Leprosy Association, Irish Foundation for Cooperative Development, Irish Missionary Union, Irish United Nations Association, Methodist Church in Ireland World Development and Relief Committee, Overseas Institute for Community Development, Trocaire, Voluntary Service International, World Health Foundation of Ireland.

Director of Consumer Affairs: J.M. Murray, 13 Hume Street, Dublin 2. Tel. (01) 603399.

Consumers' Association of Ireland: 33-35 Wicklow Street, Dublin 2. Tel. (01) 770197. *Chairperson* - Joan Morrison. A full member of the Bureau Européen des Unions des Consommateurs, Brussels.

DEVCO (State Agencies Development Cooperation Organisation): Kildress House, Pembroke Row, Dublin 2. Tel. (01) 760245. *Chairman* - Dr Tom Walsh.

HEDCO (Higher Education for Development Cooperation): Kildress House, Pembroke Row, Dublin 2. Tel. (01) 604666. *Chairman* - Professor George Dawson. *General Secretary* - Paud Murphy.

FINANCE

Department of Finance: Government Buildings, Upper Merrion Street, Dublin 2. Tel. (01) 767571. *Minister* - Alan Dukes TD. *Secretary* - Maurice Doyle.

FISHERIES

Department of Fisheries and Forestry: Leeson Lane, Dublin 2. Tel. (01) 600444. *Minister* - Paddy O'Toole TD. *Minister of State* - Michael D'Arcy TD. *Secretary* - Paddy Whooley.

Bord Iascaigh Mhara: Hume House, Ballsbridge, Dublin 4. Tel. (01) 683956 and 683977. *Chief Executive* - R.A. Meaney.

Irish Fishermen's Organisation: 16 Nassau Street, Dublin 2. Tel. (01) 715033. *Secretary General* - Frank Doyle.

Irish Fish Processors and Exporters Association: *Chairman* - Tadhg Gallagher, c/o Gallagher Brothers, Killybegs, Co. Donegal.

Irish Fish Producers' Organisation: 54 Wellington Road, Dublin 4. *Chief Executive* - Declan Tanham.

FOREIGN AFFAIRS

Department of Foreign Affairs: 80 St. Stephen's Green, Dublin 2. Tel. (01) 780822. *Minister* - Peter Barry TD. *Minister of State* - Jim O'Keeffe. *Secretary* - Sean Donlon.

INDUSTRY

UNICE (Union of Industries of the EEC - Union des Industries de la CEE): Rue de Loxum 6, Boite 21, 1000 Brussels. Tel. (16322) 5126780. *Secretary General* - Bernard Sassen. *Irish members:* Confederation of Irish Industry, Kildare Street, Dublin 2. Tel. (01) 779801. *Director General* - Liam Connellan. Federated Union of Employers, Baggot Bridge House, 84-88 Lower Baggot Street, Dublin 2. Tel. (01) 601011. *Director General* - Dan McAuley.
Liaison Officer in Brussels - Aidan O'Boyle, Bureau de Liaison auprés des Communautés Européenes, 66 Avenue de Cortenberg, Boite 3, 1040 Brussels. Tel. (16322) 7361974.

NORTHERN IRELAND

Cooperation North: 56 Fitzwilliam Square, Dublin 2. Tel. (01) 764854. *Chief Executive* - Hugh Quigley.

TRADE UNIONS

ETUC (European Trade Union Confederation - Confederation Européene des Syndicats, CES), Rue Montagne aux Herbes, Potagères 37, 1000 Brussels. Tel. (16322) 2191090. *Secretary General* - Matthias Hinterscheid. *Irish member organisation:* Irish Congress of Trade Unions, 19 Raglan Road, Dublin 2. Tel. (01) 680641. *General Secretary* - Donal Nevin.

Youth Forum of the European Communities: *Secretary General* - Ad Melkert, Avenue de Cortenberg 66, Boite 10, 1040 Brussels. Tel. 7365355.

Irish Council of the European Movement: 32 Nassau Street, Dublin 2. Tel. (01) 714300. *Director* - Catherine Cleary. *President* - Charles Haughey TD. *Vice-Presidents* - Barry Desmond TD, Senator Jim Dooge, Michael Killeen, Senator Eoin Ryan. *Chairwoman* - Katherine Meenan. *Vice-Chairman* - Sean Healy. *Hon. Secretary* - Ruairi Brugha. *Hon. Treasurer* - Peter Gilligan. The Council nominates candidates for the Robert Schuman awards. (In 1983 awards were won by Mary Hanafin and William Carroll.) It is responsible for allocating three scholarships each year, funded by the Department of Education, to the College of Europe in Bruges, Belgium, and it runs an annual competition to commemorate Michael Sweetman, a former director who died in the 1972 air crash. This competition is for vocational school pupils; prizewinners are taken on a tour to European Community countries and institutions.

Further Reading

EC = EUROPEAN COMMUNITIES
Unless otherwise stated, books listed here were published in Dublin.

Chapter 1, Community Building

Adamthwaite, Anthony, *The Lost Peace - International Relations in Europe 1918-1939*, London, Arnold, 1980.

Cooney, John, 'Sean MacBride's Contribution to European Unity', *The Irish Times*, 26 January 1984. *A United State of Europe?*, Dublin University Press, 1980.

Coughlan, Anthony, *Ireland and the Common Market: The Alternatives to Membership*, Dublin, Common Market Study Group, 1972.

Fanning, Ronan, *Independent Ireland*, Helicon, 1983.

Government White Paper, *The Accession of Ireland to the European Communities*, Laid before each House of the Oireachtas, January 1972, Stationery Office.

Hederman, Miriam, *The Road to Europe - Irish Attitudes 1948-61*, IPA, 1983.

Keogh, Dermot, 'Sources for the History of European Integration in Ireland' (1945-1955) in *Sources for the History of European Integration*, (Ed.) Walter Lipgens, European University, Florence, 1980.

Lecerf, Jean, *La Communauté en Péril*, Paris, Gallimard, 1975.

Monnet, Jean, *Memoirs*, London, Collins, 1978.

Tindemans, Leo, *European Union*, Brussels, EC, 1976.

Chapter 2, The Anatomy of the EEC

Lasok, D. & Bridges, J.W., *An Introduction to the Law and Institutions of the European Communities*, London, Butterworth, 1976.

Noel, Emile, *The European Community: How It Works*, Brussels, Commission of the EC, 1979.

Report of the 'Three Wise Men', Report on European Institutions, October 1979, Brussels, Council of the EC, 1980.

Spierenburg Report, Proposals for Reform of the Commission of the European Communities and its Services, Brussels, EC, 1979.

Sutton, Mary, *The Institutions of the EEC*, Trócaire/Irish Commission for Justice and Peace, 1976.

Tindemans, Leo, *European Union*, Brussels, EC, 1976.

Vedel Report, Report of the Ad Hoc Group to Examine the Problem of Increased Powers for the European Parliament, Luxembourg/Strasbourg, European Parliament, 1972.

Chapter 3, The European Council

Morgan, Annette, *From Summit to Council - Evolution in the EEC*, London, PEP/Chatham House, 1976.

Noel, Emile, 'Quelques Reflexions sur le Conseil Européen' in *Les Rouages de L'Europe*, Brussels, Edition Lobor, 1979.

Chapters 4 & 5, The Council of Ministers & The Commission

Dagtoglou, P. D., *Basic Problems of the European Community*, Oxford, Blackwell Press, 1975.

(For full references to the Spierenburg, Tindemans and 'Three Wise Men' reports, see Further Reading, Chapter 2.)

Chapter 6, The European Parliament

Coombes, David, *The Future of the European Parliament*, London, Policy Studies Institute, 1979.

Cooney, John, *Race for Europe*, Irish University Press, 1979.

Moxon-Browne, Edward, 'The Relationship between the Irish Parliament and the European Parliament 1973-77, in *The European Parliament and the National Parliaments*, (Ed.) Valentine Herman and Rinus Van Schendelen, Farnborough, Saxon House, 1979.

Spinelli, Altiero, *Report on the Preliminary Draft Treaty Establishing the European Union*, European Parliament Document 1-1200/83/A & B, 1983.

Vedel Report, For full reference see Further Reading, Chapter 2.

Chapter 7, The Court of Justice

Brown, L.N. & Jacobs, F.G., *The Court of Justice of the European Communities*, London, Sweet & Maxwell, 1977.

Chubb, Basil, *The Constitution and Constitutional Change in Ireland*, IPA, 1978.

Lang, John Temple, *The Common Market and Common Law*, Chicago/London, University of Chicago, 1966.

MacKenzie Stuart, A.J., *The European Communities and the Rule of Law*, London, Stevens, 1977.

Mathijsen, P.S.R.F., *A Guide to European Community Law*, London, Sweet & Maxwell, 1975.

Murphy, Finbarr, 'The European Community and the Irish Legal System' in *Ireland and the European Communities - Ten Years of Membership*, (Ed.) David Coombes, Gill and Macmillan, 1983.

Parry, A., Hardy, S. & Dinnage, J., EEC *Law*, (2nd edition), London, Sweet & Maxwell, 1981.

Chapter 8, How Decisions Are Made

Sasse, Poulet, Coombes & Deprez, (Eds.), *Decision Making in the European Community*, New York/London, Preager, 1977.

Wallace, H., *Policy Making in the European Communities*, London, John Wiley, 1977.

Chapter 9, The Budget

Laffan, Bridget, 'Budgetary Reform of the European Community' in *Administration*, Vol. 29, No. 4, p. 323.

Wallace, H., *Budgetary Politics: The Finances of the European Communities*, London, Allen & Unwin, 1980.

Chapter 10, The Common Agricultural Policy

Cox, Patrick G. & Kearney, Brendan, 'The Impact of the Common Agricultural Policy' in *Ireland and the European Communities - Ten Years of Membership*, (Ed.) David Coombes, Gill and Macmillan, 1983.

Economic and Social Research Institute, *A Review of the Common Agricultural Policy and the Implications of Modified Systems for Ireland*, Broadsheet No. 21, 1983.

Fennell, Rosemary, *The Common Agricultural Policy of the European Community - Its Institutional and Administrative Organisation*, London, Granada, 1979.

National Economic and Social Council, *Rural Areas: Change and Development*, Report No. 41, 1978.

Sheehy, Seamus J., 'The Impact of EEC Membership on Irish Agriculture' in *Journal of Agricultural Economics*, Vol. 31, No. 3, pp 279-310, 1980.

Tracy, Michael, *Agriculture in Western Europe - Challenge and Response 1880-1980*, (2nd edition), London, Granada, 1982.

Chapter 11, Fisheries

Gallagher, Eamonn, Address to the Irish Council of the European Movement on the Common Fisheries Policy, 6 May 1983.

Leigh, Michael, *European Integration and the Common Fisheries Policy*, London, Croom Helm, 1983.

Chapter 12, Industry

Albert, M. & Ball, R.J., 'Towards European Economic Recovery in the 1980s', European Parliament Working Documents 1983-1984, July 1983.

Blackwell, John & O'Malley, Eoin, 'Irish Industry' in *Ireland and the European Community*, (Ed.) P.J. Drudy and D. McAleese, Cambridge University Press, 1984.

Confederation of Irish Industry, *Grants and Incentives for Irish Industry*, 1983.

Whitaker, T.K., 'From Protection to Free Trade - The Irish Experience' in *Administration*, Vol. 21, pp 405-23, 1973.

Chapter 13, Trade

Matthews, Alan, 'The European Community's External Trade Policy: Implications for Ireland', Irish Council for the European Movement, 1980.

McAleese, Dermot, 'Changing Pattern of Trade' in *Community Report*, January 1983, Office of the European Communities, Dublin.

Chapter 14, Political Cooperation

De Schoutteete, Philippe, *La Cooperation Politique Européene*, Brussels, Collection 'Europe', 1980.

Keatinge, Patrick, *A Place among the Nations: Issues in Irish Foreign Policy*, IPA, 1978. *A Singular Stance: Irish Neutrality in the 1980's*, IPA, 1984.

MacKernan, Padraic, 'Ireland and European Political Cooperation' in *Ireland Today*, Bulletin of the Department of Foreign Affairs, No. 948, January 1982.

Salmon, Trevor C., 'Ireland: A Neutral in the Community?' in *Journal of Common Market Studies*, Vol. XX, No. 3.

Chapter 15, The Community and the Third World

Fitzpatrick, J., 'Industrialisation, Trade and Ireland's Development Co-operation Policy' in *Industrialisation, Trade, and Ireland's Development Co-Operation Policy*, Advisory Council on Development Cooperation, 1981. 'Trade between newly industrialised and newly industrialising countries: the case of Ireland' in *Administration*, Vol. 31, No. 2, 1983.

O'Brien, Declan, *Ireland and the Third World - A Study of Government Aid*, Irish Commission for Justice and Peace, 1980.

Sutton, Mary, *The Institutions of the EEC - How Development Cooperation Policy is Formulated*, Trócaire/Irish Commission for Justice and Peace, 1976. *Government Aid to the Third World - Review and Assessment*, Trócaire/Irish Commission for Justice and Peace, 1977.

Chapter 16, The European Monetary System

Irish Council for the European Movement, *European Monetary Union and the Sterling Link*, 1975.

Ludlow, Peter, *The Making of the European Monetary System*, London, Butterworth, 1982.

Chapter 17, Regional Policy

Central Statistics Office, *Household Budget Survey, 1980*, Vol. 2, February 1984, Stationery Office.

Hart, Joan & Laffan, Bridget, 'Consequences of the Community's Regional and Social Policies' in *Ireland and the European Communities*, (Ed.) David Coombes, Gill and Macmillan, 1983.

Healy, J., 'Strasbourg Notebook', *The Irish Times*, 25, 26, 27 January 1984.

Lee, Joseph, *Reflections on Ireland in the EEC*, ICEM, 1984.

MacNamara, Brendan, 'Wanted: a bigger Regional Fund' in *Community Report*, January 1983, Office of the European Communities, Dublin.

NESC, *Institutional Arrangements for Regional Economic Development*, No. 22, 1976.

Whelan, Noel, 'EIB: Key Role in Job Creation' in *Community Report*, January 1983, Office of the European Communities, Dublin.

Chapters 18 & 19, Social Affairs & Women and the EEC

ANCO, Annual Reports.

Employment Equality Agency, Annual Reports.

Hart, Joan & Laffan, Bridget, See Further Reading, Chapter 17.

O'Cearbhaill, Tadg, 'Social Fund up to Expectations' in *Community Report*, January 1983, Office of the European Communities, Dublin.

Chapter 20, The Consumer, the Environment and Culture

Doyle, G.J., 'Conserving Bogland' in *Promise and Performance - Irish Environmental Policies Analysed*, (Ed.) John Blackwell & Frank J. Convery, RECP, 1983.

European Community, *The European Community's Environmental Policy*, Brussels, European Documentation series, 1/1984.

Lang, John Temple, 'The Wildlife Act and EEC Bird Conservation Measures' in *Promise and Performance* (see under Doyle above).

189

Chapter 21, Northern Ireland

Economic and Social Committee, *Irish Border Areas*, Information Report, Brussels, 1983.

Haagerup, Neils, *Draft Report of the European Parliament Political Affairs Committee on the Situation in Northern Ireland*, Strasbourg/Luxembourg, December 1983.

Hainsworth, Paul, 'Northern Ireland: A European Role' in *Journal of Common Market Studies*, Vol. XX, No. 1, pp 1-5, September 1981. 'Direct Rule in Northern Ireland: the European Community Dimension 1972-1979' in *Administration*, Vol. 31, No. 1, p. 53, 1983.

Martin, Simone, *Report on Community Regional Policy and Northern Ireland*, European Parliament, Strasbourg/Luxembourg, May 1981.

Office of the European Commission, Northern Ireland, *The Impact of Membership*, January 1983.

Chapter 22, Administration and Politics

Barrington, T.J., *The Irish Administrative System*, IPA, 1980.

Burns, B. & Salmon, T.C., 'Policy Making Co-ordination in Ireland on European Community Issues', *Journal of Common Market Studies*, Vol. XV, No. 4, 1977.

Chubb, Basil, *Source Book of Irish Government*, IPA, 1983.

Laffan, Bridget, 'Ireland and Denmark in the European Community - Political and Administrative Aspects' in *Administration*, Vol. 29, No. 4, p. 323, 1981.

Lee, Joseph, *Reflections on Ireland in the EEC*, ICEM, 1984.

Murphy, Finbarr, 'The European Community and the Irish Legal System' in *Ireland and the European Communities - Ten Years of Membership*, (Ed.) David Coombes, Gill and Macmillan, 1983.

Scott, Dermot, 'EEC Membership and the Irish Administrative System' in *Adn.inistration*, Vol. 31, No. 2, p. 147, 1983. 'Adapting the Machinery of Central Government' in *Ireland and the European Communities* (see reference under Murphy above).

Chapter 23, The Balance Sheet

Coombes, David (Ed.), *Ireland and the European Communities - Ten Years of Membership*, Gill and Macmillan, 1983.

Cooney, John, *The EEC in Crisis*, Dublin University Press, 1979.

Lee, Joseph, 'Society and Culture' in *Unequal Achievement - The Irish Experience, 1957-1982*, (Ed.) Frank Litton, IPA, 1982. *Reflections on Ireland in the EEC*, ICEM, 1984.

National Economic & Social Council, *The Socio-Economic Position of Ireland in the European Communities*, Report No. 58, May 1981.

European Parliament, *The Effects on Ireland of Membership of the European Communities*, Luxembourg/Strasbourg, 1979.

Index

191